CHRISTIANITY AND
COMPARATIVE RELIGION

CHRISTIANITY AND COMPARATIVE RELIGION

J. N. D. ANDERSON, o.b.e., ll.d., f.b.a.

Professor of Oriental Laws, and Director of the
Institute of Advanced Legal Studies, in the University of London

INTER-VARSITY PRESS
BOX F, DOWNERS GROVE, ILLINOIS 60515

Second printing, March 1971

*This book is based on the Church of Ireland
series of theological lectures for 1970, given
at the Queen's University of Belfast, Northern Ireland.
Biblical quotations, unless otherwise indicated, are
from the Revised Standard Version of the Bible, copyright
in 1946 and 1952 by the Division of Christian Education,
National Council of the Churches of Christ in the USA.*

*Inter-Varsity Press is the book publishing
division of Inter-Varsity Christian Fellowship.*

*ISBN 0-87784-477-1
Library of Congress Catalog Card Number 73-135847*

Printed in the United States of America

CONTENTS

1 INTRODUCTION

Comparative religion is a subject which arouses a lively and widespread interest today. Strictly speaking, the very term is, of course, a solecism, for it is not 'religion' itself which is 'comparative', but the method of study and approach. But to speak of 'the comparative study of religion', or 'the comparative study of law', seems unnecessarily pedantic, although it should be stated emphatically that this is what comparative religion or comparative law really means. As such, comparative religion is simply one aspect of the study of religion.

In a book published only this year under the title of *Comparative Religion in Education*,[1] reference is made to 'the remarkable popularity of "world religions" as a subject for academic and semi-academic study in Western educational institutions. Universities, colleges of education, seminaries and theological colleges, secondary schools and part-time classes are all, in their various ways, attempting to meet what is in process of becoming a widespread popular desire for insights into the beliefs and practices of religions other than Christianity.' And Eric J. Sharpe suggests that the reasons for this 'upsurge of enthusiasm for a subject which until a few years ago remained the province of a very few specialists' can be found in improved communications with other lands, insistent questioning of the role of the West *vis-à-vis* non-Western peoples, increased availability of information on the

[1] Edited by John R. Hinnells (Oriel Press, Newcastle, 1970). In this book O. R. Johnston's essay particularly emphasizes the fact that a convinced Christian can make a distinctive contribution to this subject, and that the study of comparative religion in school or university can be constructive and helpful – rather than inimical – to Christian faith.

popular level, the presence in our midst of ever larger numbers of adherents of non-Western religious traditions, and also a growing feeling of disillusionment with organized Christianity and with the intellectual foundations of Western society, all of which have combined to 'turn increasing numbers of people – and not least young people – towards a new quest for "light from the East" '.[2] Other reasons might, of course, also be given, such as dissatisfaction with an affluent and technologically sophisticated society, an over-confident intellectual humanism or even a despair, in some quarters, as to how to make religious instruction periods interesting.

The subject is formidable in the extreme, for it has expanded so rapidly that it is often broken down today into the history of religion, the phenomenology of religion, the psychology of religion, the sociology of religion and the philosophy of religion[3] – although it must be emphasized that the phenomenological and historical study of religion are not necessarily comparative. Naturally enough, therefore, it has repeatedly been emphasized that no one scholar can ever hope to cover the whole field. This is, indeed, obvious when one realizes that, in spite of all the classical texts which have been translated into Western languages and all that has been written on the subject, it is exceedingly difficult – if not impossible – really to enter into the meaning and ethos of another religion without an intimate acquaintance with those who put that religion into practice in their daily lives and, ideally, a competent knowledge of the language or languages in which its basic literature is written. This means that we are left with only three alternatives: the first-hand assessment of a limited field by an individual scholar; a broad survey of a wide field based largely on second-hand materials; or a collaborative study by a number of different scholars.

But students of comparative religion do not differ among themselves only in their linguistic and scholarly equipment, but also in their religious convictions. Ideally, from one point of view, they should have no preconceived ideas at all and should approach the subject in an attitude of complete detachment. But while this might facilitate a ruthless objectivity,

[2] *Ibid.*, p. 1.   [3] *Ibid.*, p. 9.

it would almost certainly hinder any deep understanding; for it seems probable that the secrets of religion are almost as inaccessible to one who is himself devoid of any religious conviction as are those of music to one who is tone deaf. 'No one', as Wilfred Cantwell Smith has remarked, 'has understood the diverse faiths of mankind if his so-called explanation of them makes fundamental nonsense of each one.'[4] In any case, a complete freedom from preconceived ideas is a practical impossibility; and in my experience the unbeliever is just as much conditioned by his unbelief as the believer is by his faith.

Statistics about religious affiliation are seldom reliable. This is not only, or even primarily, because census figures are themselves often both unreliable and hard to come by, but because no census figures can throw much light on the variety of beliefs and practices which prevail in many countries or the increasing number of those who have largely rejected their ancestral faiths. Within several of the great world religions, moreover, there is a wide variety of sects and schools of thought. At a rough estimate, however, there must be some 900 million of those who belong to what is sometimes termed the 'Western Judaic Christian tradition'[5] and a comparable number made up, in roughly equal proportions, of Muslims and Hindus. There are several hundred million Buddhists, some of whom combine Confucian, Shintoist or other teachings with their Buddhism; and, by a rather different method of calculation, there are hundreds of millions of Chinese who might be classified as Communists, Confucianists, Taoists or Buddhists, and frequently combine elements from two or more of these sources. There must be some forty million Japanese adherents of Shintoism;[6] about eight million Sikhs; some two million Zoroastrians and two million Jains; perhaps one million Bahā'īs; and a very large but indeterminate number of persons who still follow some primitive or animistic[7] religion.

[4] W. Cantwell Smith, *The Faith of Other Men* (New American Library, New York: New English Library, London. Copyright 1962. First Printing, 1965), p. 13.
[5] *Cf.* H. D. Lewis and R. L. Slater, *World Religions* (C. A. Watts, 1966), p. 1, to which I am much indebted, both here and elsewhere in this book.
[6] Although a far larger number of Shintoists is sometimes claimed.
[7] It is also noteworthy that animistic beliefs and practices colour the daily

By way of introduction to the studies which will follow, it seems essential to give preliminary attention to three of the major questions which face anyone interested in comparative religion today: the insistent demands we hear from so many quarters for a syncretistic approach to the whole subject of religion; the problems – both syncretistic and otherwise – raised by the phenomenon of mysticism, whether spontaneous or induced; and the current vogue for 'dialogue', rather than 'evangelism', in our approach to men of faiths other than our own.

Syncretism

The syncretic approach – *i.e.* the attempt to unite or reconcile diverse religious tenets or practices – is exceedingly popular today. Even Christians themselves, as W. A. Visser 't Hooft justly remarks, 'give the impression that they consider Christianity as a species of the genus religion, as a sub-division of the general human preoccupation with the divine . . . Since the eighteenth century, and especially since Schleiermacher, this reduction of Christianity to a province of the wide empire of religion has become so widely accepted that most Christians are shocked and surprised when they are told that this view of Christianity is a modern invention which has no foundation whatever in the Bible. Karl Barth has said, "Neo-Protestantism is religionism", for it has systematically sought to interpret the Christian faith in categories which were taken from a general philosophy of religion rather than in categories provided by the Christian faith itself.'[8]

But is it not undeniable, most people will instinctively retort, that Christianity is a religion? If religion is defined as 'Action or conduct indicating a belief in, reverence for, and desire to please, a divine ruling power; the exercise or practice of rites or observances implying this . . . A particular system of faith and worship . . . Recognition on the part of man of some higher unseen power as having control of his destiny,

---

lives of millions who claim to be Christians, Muslims, or adherents of some other world religion. *Cf., inter alia,* S. M. Zwemer's *The Influence of Animism on Islam* (Macmillan, New York, 1920).

[8] W. A. Visser 't Hooft, *No Other Name* (SCM Press, 1963), pp. 94f.

and as being entitled to obedience, reverence, and worship;
the general mental and moral attitude resulting from this
belief . . .'[9], then it is impossible to deny that Christianity
qualifies for inclusion. So it is perfectly in order to compare
it – as I shall attempt to do in the course of these chapters –
with other religions. Clearly, if there is such a phenomenon
as a genus 'religion', then Christianity (as a convenient label
for a complex of phenomena which reflect a system of belief
associated with both worship and conduct) is a species in it,
in the same formal sense that Islam and Hinduism are. But
these labels all represent abstractions. The Christian must,
therefore, continually remind himself that no man is 'saved'
by Christianity as a religion, but only by the gospel as such
(*i.e.* the saving action of God as recorded and interpreted in
the New Testament). This is different *in kind* not only from
the non-Christian religious systems, but also from Christianity
itself, viewed as a system. Man-in-Christianity lies under the
judgment of God in the same way, and for the same reasons,
as man-in-paganism.

   The fact is that generalizations about religion are almost
always misleading. Nothing could be further from the truth
than the dictum of John Haynes Holmes that 'Religion has
not many voices, but only one', for even the most elementary
study of the different religions reveals fundamental contradictions. Most of the world's religions have, it is true, developed
an ecclesiastical hierarchy of some sort, certain rituals or
forms of worship, and also – though less universally – a
pattern of moral and ceremonial behaviour to which the
fellowship of the faithful is expected to conform. Comparative
studies in these fields by sociologists, anthropologists and
other scholars may well be valuable and instructive. But even
the most cursory examination of the theology of these different
religions reveals far more contradiction than consensus.

   We must, therefore, resist the specious argument that we
should gloss over the contradictions between one religion and
another, should take as sympathetic a view of attempts to
mix different religions as we do of attempts to mix different
races and, regarding atheism as the one enemy, should defend

[9] *Shorter Oxford English Dictionary.*

the common religious front at all costs. Loose thinking will get us nowhere. The world today is characterized not only by rampant atheism but also by an almost feverish curiosity about religion and a wistful, and sometimes frantic, quest for something which transcends mere materialism; and this longing for reality must not be fobbed off with a synthetic and misleading answer. It is, indeed, this very quest for reality, when seen in the light of the pressing need for men and women of different races, cultures and backgrounds to learn to understand each other and work together for the common good, that provides the major incentive for a syncretistic approach to religious differences, or even for the eventual emergence of one universal world-religion. But before we succumb to any such temptation we must see clearly what syncretism means.

'Real syncretism', as A. Oepke asserts, 'is always based on the presupposition that all positive religions are only reflections of a universal original religion and show therefore only gradual differences.'[1] So the syncretic approach may be defined as 'the view which holds that there is no unique revelation in history, that there are many different ways to reach the divine reality, that all formulations of religious truth or experience are by their very nature inadequate expressions of that truth and that it is necessary to harmonise as much as possible all religious ideas and experiences so as to create one universal religion for mankind'.[2]

Nor is syncretism any new phenomenon. It was found in ancient Israel, where it was vehemently denounced by the prophets. It was characteristic of Hellenism and Gnosticism, and was widespread in the Roman Empire, where the Emperor Alexander Severus 'had in his private chapel not only the statues of the deified emperors, but also those of the miracle worker Appolonius of Tyana, of Christ, of Abraham and of Orpheus'.[3] It found one of its most powerful advocates in a Muslim emperor, Akbar the Great, who tried to create a

---

[1] Quoted by W. A. Visser 't Hooft from *Das neue Gottesvolk* (1950), p. 124.
[2] W. A. Visser 't Hooft, *op. cit.*, p. 11.
[3] *Ibid.*, p. 15 – based on A. D. Nock, *Conversion* (Oxford University Press, 1933, reprinted 1961), p. 115.

new, universal religion. His vision was to bring the different religions of the Moghul empire into one, 'but in such a fashion that they should be both one and all; with the great advantage of not losing what is good in one religion, while gaining whatever is better in another. In that way, honour would be rendered to God, peace would be given to the peoples, and security to the Empire'.[4] It burst forth anew in Rousseau and Goethe, who believed that there was 'a basic religion, that of pure nature and reason, and that this is of divine origin'.[5] And the same fundamental approach is shared by such men as W. E. Hocking and Arnold Toynbee. The latter rejects 'what he calls the "argument" of the Christian Church that it is unique in virtue of the uniqueness of Christ and of his incarnation. It is not credible that "God who is another name for love and who is believed to have demonstrated his love for Man by becoming incarnate in a human being, will have done this self-sacrificing deed of emptying himself at one time and place and one only." What remains are the teachings of Christianity. But these are not exclusively Christian. For the idea of God's self-sacrifice is found in ancient nature-worship and in Buddhism.'[6]

Here the fundamental fallacy is that Hocking, Toynbee and a multitude of other writers tend to interpret Christianity 'wholly in terms of ideas', rather than God's decisive intervention in history. 'But Christianity is not a philosophical system; it is, as Lesslie Newbigin says, "primarily news and only secondarily views." And if the news is denied the views hang in the air.'[7]

There have been a number of recent manifestations of syncretism also in the East – quite apart from the fact that Hinduism, and indeed the traditional religions of Africa and much of Asia, are syncretistic in their very nature. Thus the great Hindu mystic Rāmakrishna 'would speak of himself as the same soul that had been born before as Rāma, as Krishna, as Jesus or as Buddha'. His teachings were propagated by Swami Vivekānanda, who appealed, at the World's Parliament of Religions in Chicago in 1893, that those present should proclaim to the world that all paths lead to the same God, and

[4] *Ibid.*, p. 36. [5] *Ibid.*, pp. 24ff. [6] *Ibid.*, p. 35. [7] *Loc. cit.*

who exclaimed: 'May he who is the Brahma of the Hindus, the Ahura Mazda of the Zoroastrians, the Buddha of the Buddhists, the Jehovah of the Jews, the Father in Heaven of the Christians, give strength to you to carry out your noble idea.'[8]

It was thus that Gandhi insisted that 'The need of the moment is not one religion, but mutual respect and tolerance of the different religions. . . . . Any attempt to root out traditions, effects of heredity, etc., is not only bound to fail, but is a sacrilege. The soul of religions is one, but it is encased in a multitude of forms. The latter will persist to the end of time . . . Truth is the exclusive property of no single scripture . . . I cannot ascribe exclusive divinity to Jesus. He is as divine as Krishna or Rama or Mahomed or Zoroaster.'[9]

Syncretic sects and movements have burgeoned, in recent years, from the soil of many different religions. Such, from a Hindu background, are the Rāmakrishna Mission and the Theosophical movement, the aim of which is 'to rescue from degradation the archaic truths which are the basis of all religions; and to uncover the fundamental unity from which they all spring'.[1] Such, too – from a Muslim origin – is Bahā'ism, for the nine doors through which men may enter the great Bahā'ī temple in Wilmette, near Chicago, represent the 'nine religions of the world', which all find in the Bahā'ī faith the essence of their own belief and the definitive revelation of ultimate reality. Syncretic movements can also be found in Japan, where the symbol of Ittoen, the Garden of Light, is a 'swastika with a cross at the centre and a sun in the background', and whose prayer is, 'Teach us to worship the essence of all religions, and help us to learn the one ultimate truth.'[2] It is clear, moreover, that Spiritualism, in so far as it has been developed as a specific religious movement, has definitely syncretistic features. And Visser 't Hooft points out that even Moral Rearmament, by preaching 'change' without specifying the religious content of that change, contributes to the syncretistic confusion of our time.[3]

---

[8] *Ibid.*, p. 38.   [9] E. C. Dewick, *The Christian Attitude to Other Religions* (Cambridge University Press, 1953), p. 20.
[1] *Ibid.*, p. 21.   [2] W. A. Visser 't Hooft, *op. cit.*, pp. 43, 45.   [3] *Ibid.*, p. 48.

Syncretism, then, is a continually recurrent phenomenon. One of its comparatively recent apostles was, indeed, D. H. Lawrence, who himself described *Lady Chatterley's Lover* as 'frankly and faithfully a phallic novel', which seeks to resuscitate the spirit of the ancient fertility cults. But the acme of Lawrence's syncretism is to be found in *The Man Who Died*, where he goes so far as to depict the risen Christ as discovering true life when he embraces the priestess of the temple of Isis, and says, 'This is the great atonement, the being in touch. The gray sea and the rain, the wet narcissus and the woman I wait for, the invisible Isis and the unseen sun are all in touch and at one.'[4] And a somewhat similar approach characterizes a recent book by John Allegro, *The Sacred Mushroom and the Cross*, which has been given an unwarranted degree of publicity and attention in the press. Here again we find the same emphasis on the phallic motif, the same reckless indulgence in imagination and the same utter disregard of all evidence to the contrary, but this time with the paraphernalia of scholarship. We also find an obsession with the hallucinogenic properties of a certain mushroom to which passing reference is made below.[5]

Visser 't Hooft justly remarks that syncretism, in many different forms, has 'the same basic motifs . . . Thus we hear a hundred times in all languages that there are many ways to God and that God is too great,[6] too unknowable to reveal himself in a single revelation and once for all. Syncretism is thus essentially a revolt against the uniqueness of revelation

[4] D. H. Lawrence, *The Man Who Died* (Secker, 1931), p. 148.
[5] It must be left to an expert in Semitic philology to write an authoritative refutation of this strange book. I shall content myself with observing:

(1) that I am informed by first-rank Semitic scholars – Christian, Jewish and agnostic – that Mr Allegro's philological arguments are, at best, dubious in the extreme;

(2) that to suggest that the Gospels – with all their ethical teaching, and those parables, disputes, *etc.*, which are accepted by the most radical critics as historical – were in fact composed as secret eulogies of the properties of a 'sacred mushroom' or of some fertility cult seems to betray an obsession with drugs and sex and a positive flight from history – *e.g.* in Mr Allegro's strange indifference to the evidence provided by passages in the Epistles such as 1 Corinthians 15 (see pp. 34ff. below) or by references to Jesus and the crucifixion in sources other than the New Testament.

[6] Although not in the writings of men such as Lawrence and Allegro.

in history. True universality, it claims, can only be gained if the pretension that God has actually made himself definitely known in a particular person and event at a particular time is given up.' But a God who 'speaks in an infinite variety of ways, but never decisively, really throws man back upon himself, for it is then up to man to determine how and where he can reach ultimate truth. Thus the syncretisms conceive of religion as a system of insights and concepts rather than as a dialogical relation between a personal God and his creature. They all tend to some form of gnosis, sometimes of a more rationalistic kind, sometimes more intuitive or esoteric. They seek to realize salvation rather than to receive it. In this way they are, often unwittingly, contradicting their own claim to universality. For they in fact exclude those religions for which the revelation of a personal God is the central category.'[7]

In this quest for ultimate truth Lesslie Newbigin emphasizes what Nicol Macnicol calls 'the great divide among the religions': namely, their attitude to history. 'There are in principle two ways in which one can seek unity and coherence behind or beyond all the multiplicity and incoherence which human experience presents to us. One way is to seek unity as an existent reality behind the multiplicity of phenomena . . .' – and this, Newbigin says, is typified in the wheel. 'The cycle of birth, growth, decay and death through which plants, animals, human beings and institutions all pass suggests the rotating wheel – ever in movement yet ever returning upon itself. The wheel offers a way of escape from this endless and meaningless movement. One can find a way to the centre where all is still, and one can observe the ceaseless movement without being involved in it. There are many spokes connecting the circumference with the centre. The wise man will not quarrel about which spoke should be chosen. Any one will do, provided it leads to the centre. Dispute among the different "ways" of salvation is pointless; all that matters is that those who follow them should find their way to that timeless, motionless centre where all is peace . . .'[8]

Here, many believe, we can discern the shadowy image of

[7] W. A. Visser 't Hooft, op. cit., pp. 48f.
[8] L. Newbigin, The Finality of Christ (SCM Press, 1969), pp. 65f.

the world religion of the future. Thus Lawrence Hyde writes: 'Amidst all the conflicts and confusions, the sympathetic observer can trace the emerging outlines of a new form of religion . . . what may prove to be the ground-plan of the Temple in which our spiritual descendants are destined to worship. The structure which thus discloses itself is *absolutely fundamental* – that of that Wisdom Religion which *by a metaphysical necessity* must provide the interior key to all exterior symbolisations and observances. It is the Way which leads back to Origin and it follows "the Pattern of the Cross".'[9] But E. C. Dewick points out that this last phrase does not refer to the cross as interpreted in historic Christianity, for Mr Hyde continues: 'The great majority of those who are finding their way back to religion, from scepticism and materialism, are not returning to the faith of their fathers, but to some form of Wisdom Religion . . . The Neo-Gnostic interprets the Incarnation as a process everlastingly being accomplished within the souls of all men and women; and from this he derives a wonderful sense of exaltation; it enables him to feel mystically one with every child of God.'

But the fundamental fact about the incarnation is that it was a unique, historical event in which God himself intervened decisively in the world he had created. It is precisely at this point that the Christian must of necessity part company with a great deal that is included under the comprehensive umbrella of mysticism. This phenomenon is found in so many different religions – and is, indeed, often expressed in such similar terms – that it frequently appears as an emotional or intuitive form of syncretism. As such, it must briefly engage our attention in this context. But before we turn to any consideration of mysticism we must cast a brief glance at the other side of Macnicol's 'great divide' – the symbol of which, Newbigin tells us, is not a wheel but a road. Life is a journey, a pilgrimage. 'The movement in which we are involved is not meaningless movement; it is movement towards a goal.' And along that road there lie a whole succession of historical events: chief among which are, of course, the incarnation, the cross and

[9] L. Hyde, *The Wisdom Religion Today* (Burning-Glass Paper, No. 13) as quoted in E. C. Dewick, *The Christian Attitude to Other Religions*, p. 19.

the resurrection. There are, moreover, innumerable points at which the traveller must choose between two or more alternative paths. And the 'goal, the ultimate resting-place, the experience of coherence and harmony, is not to be had save at the end of the road. The perfect goal is not a timeless reality hidden now behind the multiplicity and change which we experience; it is yet to be achieved.'[1]

Mysticism

Mysticism is a comprehensive word which means different things to different people. In general terms it represents the belief that direct knowledge of God, of spiritual truth or ultimate reality, is attainable 'through immediate intuition or insight and in a way differing from ordinary sense perception or the use of logical reasoning'.[2] Broadly speaking, there seem to be two main types of mysticism. The one is essentially introvertive, in which the mystic 'by turning inwards on his own consciousness and experience, and by stressing the necessity for discarding from his mind all visual or concrete images, comes to realise in a peculiarly coercive way his essential oneness with ultimate reality'.[3] The other, which may be termed extrovertive, is 'closely akin to the experience of the poet and the prophet', and is linked with some objective experience or circumstance – or with what the early Christian Fathers called the 'mystery'.

This second type of mysticism may, it is clear, be distinctively Christian. In the early church it seems that mystical experience was almost always associated with something factual or concrete; e.g. with the written words of Scripture or the action of the liturgy. 'The sign, the concrete event or situation, or piece of Scripture, and the thing signified were taken as inseparable. This patristic type of mysticism is a genuine mysticism and at the same time is completely compatible with Christian belief in an historical incarnation.'[4]

But the reason why mysticism must concern us in this context is the close connection that it can have with syncretism. This is partly because mystics, from whatever religion

[1] L. Newbigin, op. cit., pp. 65f.   [2] Webster's New Collegiate Dictionary.
[3] A Dictionary of Christian Theology, edited by Alan Richardson (SCM Press, 1969). Article on 'Mysticism' by E. J. Tinsley.   [4] Ibid., p. 225.

or background they come, are apt to speak the same sort of language, and partly because mystics in different religious traditions often recognize in each other a common experience which, they assert, transcends their theological differences. So the question inevitably arises as to whether this phenomenon does in fact provide evidence for an ultimate reality which lies behind the formulations of all religions and represents the truth that they are all trying, however imperfectly, to proclaim. How otherwise can we account for the evidence, from so many different traditions, of mystical experiences which, however much they may differ in form and depth, seem – at first sight, at least – recognizably to belong to the same family or genus?

Part of the explanation of this phenomenon assuredly lies in the philosophy and discipline which mystics from different religions often have in common. Thus in the field with which I am myself best acquainted – Muslim mysticism – we find that Neo-platonic concepts (or Neo-platonic concepts popular-ized by the pseudo 'Dionysius the Areopagite') provide the basic philosophy and technique, and that this is often com-bined with a pantheistic or monistic pattern of thought which emanates from India. Thus the mystic fervently aspires to wean his heart and mind from the phenomenal world and to realize his unity with the Infinite.

It is also important to note what has been termed 'The unbroken line of continuity in the history of "provoked mysticism" ' or techniques designed to induce states of mystical consciousness. To attain such states men have 'willingly sub-mitted themselves to elaborate ascetic procedures . . . They have practised fasting, flagellation, and sensory deprivation, and, in so doing, may have attained to states of heightened mystical consciousness, but also have succeeded in altering their body chemistry. Recent physiological investigations . . . tend to confirm the notion that provoked alterations in body chemistry and body rhythm are in no small way responsible for the dramatic changes in consciousness attendant upon these practices.'[5] Muslim dervishes, for example, have

[5] R. E. L. Masters and Jean Houston, *The Varieties of Psychedelic Experience* (Holt, Rinehart and Winston, New York, 1966), pp. 248f.

regularly attained an ecstatic state, or at least a condition of auto-hypnosis, by controlled breathing, regulated rhythm, chanting, dancing, whirling or the long maintenance of profound concentration. Similarly, devotees of both Yoga and Zen-Buddhism meticulously follow their respective systems of posture, breathing and meditation.[6]

Drugs of various sorts have also been used for such purposes for centuries. Such may, indeed, have been the nature of the *soma* of the Vedic sacrifice[7]; such is the *peyote* of the Mazatec Indians of Mexico, Indian tribes in the United States and Canada and even of the 'Native American Church'[8]; and such, according to R. G. Wassan, is a hallucinogenic mushroom known in South America, among shamanistic tribes in Siberia, and elsewhere[9] – while derivatives of hemp, datura, henbane, *etc.*, have been still more widely used.[1] More recently, 'the historic sacrality of the visionary vegetables has . . . given way to the modern notoriety of the synthetic derivatives – especially LSD, psilocybin, and mescaline'.[2] It was the publication of Aldous Huxley's *Doors of Perception* in 1954 which first popularized the use of what we may term psychedelic drugs for such purposes. There can be no doubt that while these drugs often induce a psychotic experience of panic, terror, paranoid distrust, delusions, toxic confusion and depression, they can also be used to uncover what is termed psychodynamic

---

[6] *Cf.* E. G. Parrinder, *An Introduction to Asian Religions* (SPCK, 1957), pp. 47, 123; R. C. Zaehner, *Mysticism, Sacred and Profane* (Oxford University Press, 1957), pp. 55, 95, 138, *etc.* Compare also the *kirtan*, or rhythmical singing of hymns (sometimes to the accompaniment of dancing) in some Hindu sects of *bhakti* persuasion.

[7] R. C. Zaehner, *op. cit.*, p. 3; R. E. L. Masters and J. Houston, *op. cit.*, p. 250.

[8] *Cf.* R. C. Zaehner, *op. cit.*, pp. 23f.; R. E. L. Masters and J. Houston, *op. cit.*, pp. 39ff. In this Church a pagan rite has been given a 'Christian' form and expression.

[9] R. E. L. Masters and J. Houston, *op. cit.*, pp. 250f., *etc.* But the properties of the fly agaric mushroom (*Amanita muscaria*) seem to have been much exaggerated by Wassan, and to have become an obsession with Allegro. There is no evidence at all, it seems, that this mushroom has ever grown in Judaea or the neighbourhood of Qumran, while a botanist at the Royal Botanical Gardens at Kew has stated that 'for its use as an inspiration for writers, philosophers or even rabble-rousers in Western Asia there is not one particle of evidence'.

[1] *Ibid.*, pp. 37ff.   [2] *Ibid.*, p. 252.

material from a patient's unconscious mind.[3] They also some-times have what may be called a *cognitive* or *aesthetic* effect, the former characterized by particularly lucid thought and the latter by increased sensory perception, although the records of what patients actually say when under the influence of these drugs seem to substantiate the latter much more than the former – or a riot of aesthetic stimuli rather than any lucidity of rational thought. But the problem, in this context, is whether or not these drugs may also stimulate transcendental or mystical experiences.

A reasonably convincing case can be made out for the fact that experimental psychedelic experiences *sometimes* seem to betray the seven common characteristics of introvertive mystical states of mind which W. T. Stace tabulates as evidenced by a wide sampling of the literature of mystical experience.[4] These are (1) a Unitary Consciousness, or 'a sense of cosmic oneness through positive ego transcendence'[5]; (2) a sense of being 'non-spatial and non-temporal', or the transcendence of space and time; (3) a sense of 'objectivity or reality'; (4) feelings of 'blessedness, joy, peace, happiness, *etc.*'; (5) a feeling that what is apprehended is 'holy, sacred or divine'; (6) paradoxi-cality; (7) an allegation that what they experience is 'ineffable' and impossible to describe – although Pahnke shrewdly observes that most of those who insist on this ineffability 'do in fact make elaborate attempts to communicate the experi-ence'.[6] It is also sometimes alleged that these experiences, although themselves transient, result in 'positive changes in attitudes and behaviour'.

This may well be true. But the basic question, for the Christian, is what is the origin and source of these mystical experiences, whether they are spontaneous, aided or provoked by ascetic practices, or even induced by hallucinogenic vegetables or drugs. But this must largely depend on what the mystic is primarily concerned to achieve: is this to concentrate

[3] *Cf.* W. N. Pahnke, 'L.S.D. and Religious Experience' in *L.S.D.: Man' Drugs and Society.* Edited by R. C. DeBold and R. C. Leaf (Faber and Faber, 1969), pp. 6off.
[4] W. T. Stace, *Mysticism and Philosophy* (Macmillan, 1961), pp. 110f., as quoted by R. E. L. Masters and J. Houston, *op. cit.*, p. 302.
[5] W. N. Pahnke, *loc. cit.*, p. 63. [6] *Ibid.* Contrast St Paul in 2 Cor. 12:4.

his attention on himself, on the phenomenal world (as in 'nature mysticism'), or on God? Here the first two categories of mysticism are united in being non-theistic, although sharply divided in so far as one is introverted and the other extroverted – with the result that they differ widely in their appropriate psychological techniques. But even those mystics whose ultimate aspiration is to know and enjoy God may themselves be subdivided into those who seek him through the medium of their own hearts, those who seek him through the medium of nature, and those who seek him directly, without any medium whatever. And it is significant, I think, that the great Christian mystical theologians – and, indeed, some of the leading Muslim *Ṣūfīs*[7] – would say that, in the highest mystical experience, any absorption with oneself or with nature must be no more than transitional stages to an exclusive concentration on God, and that any direct experience of him can never be reached by the mystic's own efforts, but only as a gift from God himself.[8]

If, then, we ask what is the origin and source of mystical experiences – real or alleged – as a whole, the answer must be that an enormous proportion of them have their origin in the subconscious mind of the person concerned;[9] that they must sometimes be regarded as a Satanic delusion rather than any form of divine revelation;[1] and that they are clearly sometimes of God – although I should myself be distinctly doubtful of this when they are chemically induced. It seems to me significant that while the rhapsodies of those under the influence of LSD or similar drugs often speak of ultimate reality, of cosmic unity, or sometimes of God (in very general or vividly aesthetic terms), even those who come from within the traditions of Christendom seldom speak in any meaningful way of the historic Christ.[2] But it is surely basic to true

---

[7] *E.g.* al-Qushayrī, Junayd of Baghdad, *etc.* Cf. R. C. Zaehner, *Mysticism, Sacred and Profane*, pp. 85ff.

[8] *Cf.* Col. 2:16–20. I am much indebted, in this context, to most helpful suggestions made by my friend Professor E. L. Mascall, of King's College, London.

[9] *Cf.* R. E. L. Masters and J. Houston, *op. cit.*, p. 256; R. C. Zaehner, *op. cit.*, pp. xv, 3, 39–41, 57, 59, 62, 92, *etc.*

[1] *Cf.* R. E. L. Masters and J. Houston, *op. cit.*, pp. 39, 252, *etc.*

[2] A *possible* exception to this may be found in the Native American Church. *Cf.* R. E. L. Masters and J. Houston, *op. cit.*, p. 251.

Christianity that it is only 'in the face of Jesus Christ' that the glory of God is *adequately* revealed. The great Christian mystics would themselves concur in emphasizing that Christian faith is firmly based on God's self-revelation in history, accepted in faith and repentance and translated into daily living, and that supernatural love (which can be known and enjoyed through the ordinary means of grace) is of much more importance than any mystical experience.

All the same, there are reasons other than those to which we have already referred which may explain, in part, how even mystics of the introvertive type often seem to speak somewhat the same language and to apprehend *something* of what the Christian finds in Christ. The first of these is that the mystic who 'turns inward on his own consciousness and experience' commonly believes that there, in his own heart, lies the 'image of God', ready for him to behold it, if only he can cleanse that heart – and, indeed, the eye with which he looks – from the dross of false values and from absorption in the material and the finite. And this is indeed, in some degree, perfectly true. As Dr William Temple put it: 'Because man is made in the image of God, the attempt to find God through penetrating to the inmost recesses of the self leads in men of all times and races to a similar experience. God truly is the spring of life in our souls; so to seek that spring is to seek Him; and to find it would be to find Him. But this can never quite happen. The image of God in man is defaced by sin, that is by self-will. The mind which seeks to reach that image is distorted by sin, and moulded both for good and for evil by tradition. The *via negativa* of the mystics cannot be perfectly followed. To rely on a supposedly direct communion with God in detachment from all external aids is to expose the soul to suggestions arising from its distortion as well as to those arising from the God whom it would apprehend. Mediation there must be; imagery there must be. If we do not deliberately avail ourselves of the true Mediator, the "express image" (Hebrews i, 3), we shall be at the mercy of some unworthy medium and of a distorted image.'[3] In addition, before we

[3] William Temple, *Readings in St. John's Gospel*, First Series (Macmillan, 1943), p. 92. *Cf.* also G. Campbell Morgan, *The Crises of the Christ* (Pickering

can see God even in Christ we need the quickening and illumination of the Holy Spirit.

Yet again, we shall argue in the last chapter of this book that, whenever the Spirit of God brings a man, whatever his religious background, to realize something of his sin or need, and to cry out to God for mercy, there is good reason to believe that he will in fact find that mercy where it is always and only available – at the cross of Christ – and that he will be accepted and forgiven on the basis of what God himself did at that cross to make possible the forgiveness of the repentant sinner. If this is true, then it follows that those mystics from other religious traditions who have genuinely sought the face of God – as some of them undoubtedly have – with a real sense of sin and need, have in all probability experienced his grace and forgiveness in Christ, little though they may have understood it. But this, by definition, applies to those whom R. C. Zaehner calls 'theistic' mystics rather than 'nature mystics' or even 'monistic mystics'[4] – unless, of course, some of these in fact desert their own techniques and concepts and begin to seek God himself, or God directly intervenes and breaks through.

The fact remains, however, that while 'mysticism as a system of practice and thought is central for India', it is 'marginal for Christianity'.[5] Thus E. L. Allen, after quoting W. T. Stace's somewhat morbid summary of religion as 'the desire to break away from being and existence altogether, to get beyond existence into nothingness where the great light is. It is the desire to be utterly free from the fetters of being. For every being is a fetter. Existence is a fetter. To be is to be tied to what you are. Religion is the hunger for the non-being which yet is',[6] pertinently asks what this has in common with the Sermon on the Mount or Wesley's hymns[7] – or, we might add, St Paul's passionate desire 'to know Christ, to experience the power of his resurrection, and to share his sufferings, in growing conformity with his death'.[8] This

and Inglis, 1945), pp. 29ff.   [4] R. C. Zaehner, *op. cit.*, pp. 28ff., 153ff.
[5] E. L. Allen, *Christianity among the Religions* (Allen and Unwin, 1960), p. 110.
[6] W. T. Stace, *Time and Eternity* (Oxford University Press, 1952), p. 5.
[7] E. L. Allen, *op. cit.*, p. 111.   [8] Phil. 3:10, NEB.

fundamental Christian aspiration may, moreover, be interpreted both in terms of practical daily living and in those of truly Christian mysticism.

In true Christianity nothing can ever displace the concrete, historical figure of Jesus Christ from the central place. It is, indeed, significant that in Aldous Huxley's *Perennial Philosophy* the only form of Christianity which receives favourable mention is radical mysticism which, he says, 'went some way towards liberating Christianity from its unfortunate servitude to historic fact' and presents in its place 'a spiritualized and universalized Christianity'. He regrets, however, that even in it 'the pure Perennial Philosophy has been overlaid, now more, now less, by an idolatrous preoccupation with events and things . . . regarded not merely as useful means, but as ends, intrinsically sacred and indeed divine'.[9]

As for those mystics who go beyond all this and even claim that they have attained complete union, and identification, with God – such as Meister Eckhart and Angelus Silesius among Christians, and Abū Yazīd, Ḥallāj and several others among Muslim mystics[1] – we do well to pay heed to H. D. Lewis's sober words: 'We are not meant to be God . . . but we have every solace in knowing the love of God for us and our abiding destiny in our abiding relation to Him . . . Christianity has in this way the Jesus of History at the centre of it. It is a position He is never to vacate. This is the radical difference between Christianity and other religions which have much in common with it.'[2] St Paul sums up the experience to which Christians aspire when he says: 'I have been crucified with Christ; it is no longer I who live, but Christ who lives in me; and the life I now live in the flesh I live by faith in the Son of God, who loved me and gave himself for me'[3]; or, again, when he prays for the Ephesians that Christ may dwell in their hearts by faith, and that they may be 'strong to grasp, with all God's people, what is the breadth and length and height and depth of the love of Christ, and to know it,

[9] A. Huxley, *The Perennial Philosophy* (Chatto and Windus, 1946), p. 63; *cf.* W. A. Visser 't Hooft, *No Other Name*, pp. 89f.
[1] R. C. Zaehner, *op. cit.*, p. 92.
[2] H. D. Lewis and R. L. Slater, *World Religions*, pp. 190, 196.
[3] Gal. 2:20, RSV.

though it is beyond knowledge'.[4] This is what Jesus himself meant when he spoke of the mutual abiding of Christ (and, indeed, of God the Father) and his disciples. As Visser 't Hooft puts it: 'A Christianity which should think of itself as one of many diverse contributions to the religious life of mankind is a Christianity that has lost its foundation in the New Testament.'[5] For it is of the very essence of New Testament Christianity that it goes back, again and again and again, to God's self-disclosure in the man Christ Jesus, to the atonement he made on the cross, and to the fact of the resurrection. To attempt to enter, ever more deeply, into the meaning of this historic revelation, and the present experience of the living Christ, is central to the Christian life. To try to go beyond it is false and misleading.[6]

Dialogue

Neither the Christian church nor the individual Christian can, therefore, participate in anything which savours of syncretism. For myself, moreover, I would include under this heading those 'multi-religious' services in which passages are read from a number of scriptures as though they were all on the same level. The church does not – and must not – apologize for the fact that it regards Jesus Christ as wholly unique; and that it wants all men to know him and to follow him. Its God-given calling is to proclaim the gospel to 'every creature'.

Inevitably, men of other religions will, sometimes at least, regard this as a mark of intolerance and arrogance – and we must humbly acknowledge that those who have carried the gospel to men of other faiths have all too often, in their frail humanity, been characterized by a spirit singularly out of keeping with the message they brought. Their attitude should always have been that of St Paul, who proclaimed with one breath both that *all* men should accept the glorious news that 'Christ Jesus came into the world to save sinners', and that he himself stood more in need of this salvation than anyone else.[7] Sin is, in fact, a universal sickness, and man's deepest need is

[4] Eph. 3:17, 18, NEB.
[5] W. A. Visser 't Hooft, *No Other Name*, p. 117.
[6] *Cf.* 2 Jn. 9. [7] 1 Tim. 1:15.

to understand this and to find the cure. If one of the innumerable groups of scientists and doctors who are searching, year in and year out, for the key which will unlock the door to the discovery of the causes and cure of cancer were suddenly, through no brilliance of their own, to chance upon this secret, would they forbear to share what they had found with others because of a fear that these others might regard them as arrogant or intolerant?

But the imperative duty of the Christian to proclaim the evangel does not mean that he must always indulge in monologue and that there is no place for any form of dialogue with those of other faiths. Nor does this merely mean that the non-Christian has a perfect right to answer back, as it were, and that argument must often take the place of unilateral proclamation. True 'dialogue' is by no means a synonym for argument. Its very essence is the desire to listen as well as to talk, to reach mutual understanding rather than to impose one's own ideas.

But this does not mean that the Christian participant in dialogue – or, indeed, the non-Christian participant – must compromise his distinctive testimony. As Visser 't Hooft has put it: 'Martin Buber, who has given us what is probably the most profound analysis of the nature of dialogue, has made it very clear that the presupposition of genuine dialogue is not that the partners agree beforehand to relativise their own convictions, but that they accept each other as persons. In order to enter into a deep relationship with a person the essential requirement is not that he agrees with me, that I agree with him, or that we are both willing to negotiate a compromise, but rather that I turn to him with the willingness to listen to him, to understand him, to seek mutual enrichment. I do not impose my personality on him but put myself at his disposal with all that I am. As a Christian I cannot do this without reporting to him what I have come to know about Jesus Christ. I shall make it clear that I consider my faith not as an achievement, but as a gift of grace, a gift which excludes all pride, but which obliges me to speak gratefully of this Lord to all who will hear it. I shall be glad also to listen to my partner and may learn much from his account of his spiritual journey.

The dialogue will be all the richer, if both of us give ourselves as we are. For the Christian that giving must include witness. It is possible for convinced Christians to enter into true dialogue with convinced Hindus or Muslims or Jews, yes and even syncretists, without giving up their basic convictions. It should be done in the attitude which Hocking has so well defined as "reverence for reverence". The fact that Christians believe that they know the source of divine truth does not mean that they have nothing to learn from men of other faiths. Those of us who have had the privilege of participating in such conversations have often found ourselves humbled and challenged by the evidence we have seen of true devotion, of unflinching loyalty to the truth as they see it among the adherents of other religions.'[8]

In such dialogue a clear distinction will inevitably have to be made between what we may term 'empirical Christianity' and the gospel. What Christians have made of their faith – or even of the gospel – is wide open to criticism; and we must always be ready to acknowledge this. Indeed, one of the most obvious enrichments for the Christian participant in dialogue is a new apprehension of the difference between the essential gospel and its incarnation in empirical Christianity. But we must equally allow the non-Christian participant to distinguish between the essence of his faith and its empirical manifestations. And this is precisely what we all too often fail to do. As Klostermaier puts it: 'He who has understood the meaning of dialogue will not want to have anything more to do with academic dalliance or a science of comparative religion, behaving as if it stood above all religions. He will also not want to know anything more of a certain kind of theology that works "without presuppositions" and pleases itself in manipulating definitions and formulas and forgets about man, who is the main concern. He will be more and more pulled into what is called "spirituality": the real life of the mind. I wanted to see a famous man in Benares, a sagacious philosopher, feared by many as a merciless critic of Christian theology. I had my own reasons for paying him a visit. He was polite, invited me for tea and then mounted the attack. I let him

[8] W. A. Visser 't Hooft, *op. cit.*, pp. 117f.

talk his fill, without saying a word myself. Then I started to talk about the things I had begun to understand within the dialogue – quite positively Christian. We got into a sincere, good, deep discussion. He had intended to send me away after ten minutes. When I left after two hours, he had tears in his eyes. . . .'[9]

Or again: 'The real dialogue takes place in an ultimate, personal depth; it does not have to be a talking about religion. But something does distinguish real dialogue: the challenge. Dialogue challenges both partners, takes them out of the security of their own prisons their philosophy and theology have built for them, confronts them with reality, with truth . . . a truth that demands all . . . All of a sudden the shallowness of all religious routine was laid bare, the compromise with the world, that which is essentially un-Christian in so many things that bear Christ's name . . . If dialogue is taken seriously, Christianity must be deeply sincere and upright – different from what it is now.'[1]

These quotations vividly portray the essential difference between true dialogue and either straight evangelism or theological argument. But they also demonstrate that the clear-cut line that some would draw between dialogue and evangelism is itself misleading; for the Christian participant must of necessity speak of Christ and what he means to him – and he may, at any moment, find that the dialogue has undergone a metamorphosis, and that he is pointing his friend to the one who alone can meet man's deepest needs.

Finally, I must conclude this Introduction by two personal observations. First, there is only one non-Christian religion which I can myself claim to have studied first-hand – that is, in its original language and indigenous setting. For the rest, I have had to content myself with a study of secondary material, and with the help of expert colleagues who have been kind enough to read my manuscript and have done their best to eliminate my mistakes. Secondly, I make no pretensions whatever to an attitude of religious detachment. On the contrary, the very title given to the original series of lectures on which

[9] K. Klostermaier, *Hindu and Christian in Vrindaban* (SCM Press, 1969), pp. 98f.   [1] *Ibid.*, pp. 102f.

this book is based – 'Christianity among the World's Religions'
– emphasizes my primary interest in the Christian faith. But I
have done my best to ensure that every statement I have made
about other religions is factually correct. The method I have
adopted inevitably means that I have not dealt with any
religion adequately or as a whole; for how can one summarize
in a few paragraphs, and in a study focused first on one point
and then on another, any tradition that has moved 'millions
of persons through many centuries – won their loyalty and
awe, inspired their poetry and courage, preyed upon their
gullibility and excused their foibles, teased their intellects and
warmed their hearts'?[2] I am also sadly conscious that some
of the quotations I have included, while they provide a valid
and poignant illustration of one aspect of the religion concerned,
inevitably give a one-sided picture of the religion as a whole;
and this is particularly true of Hinduism, of which Hindus
themselves are apt to say that there are as many facets of the
truth as there are persons to perceive it. But I have tried
always to remember, in the words of Wilfred Cantwell
Smith, that we must not 'fool ourselves into thinking that we
can love a Hindu or a Hottentot if we refuse to take seriously
what is his most precious possession, his faith, and if we are
supercilious about the tradition through which he finds and
nourishes it'.[3]

[2] W. Cantwell Smith, *The Faith of Other Men*, p. 18.
[3] *Ibid.*, p. 87.

2 A UNIQUE PROCLAMATION?

We shall take as our starting-point in our study of 'Christianity and Comparative Religion' the *kerygma*, or proclamation, of the apostolic church, for about this there can be no uncertainty whatever. It is unmistakably clear from the New Testament that Jesus of Nazareth was proclaimed by the apostles as a divine Saviour, and that the very basis of the apostolic message was his death and resurrection. The one who brought the divine word had himself become the divine Logos of the Fourth Gospel; for in the *kerygma* (as we find it in the Epistles, the Acts and the Revelation) the messenger has become the message, and his death, resurrection and second advent have become the essence of the proclamation.[1] Thus the heart of the apostolic teaching was that in Jesus God had intervened in human history in a way which was both sufficient and final, for Christ had died 'once for all'[2] for our sins, had been buried, and had risen from the grave on the third day.[3]

It is these unique events narrated in the Gospels which, as H. D. Lewis reminds us, form the core of the Christian faith. And he insists that they 'are not to be taken as mere symbols of something beyond them, whether in depths of our own experience or in the absolute being of God. They are not just pictures, but supreme religious reality. The Christian faith, as a distinctive faith, cannot survive the surrender of particularity. It stands or falls with the insistence that it was God himself, in the form of a man, who trod this earth two thousand years

---

[1] *Cf.* Günther Bornkamm, 'The Significance of the Historical Jesus for Faith' in *What can we know about Jesus?*, translated by G. Foley (St Andrew Press, 1969), pp. 81, 70.
[2] *Cf.* Heb. 10:10; 9:28; *etc.*   [3] 1 Cor. 15:3, 4.

ago, and died between thieves on a cross.'[4] Both the deity of
Jesus and the efficacy of his atoning death were, moreover,
proved for the apostles by the fact of his resurrection. From
the first the confident assertion that Jesus had been raised
from death was the basis and starting-point of their proclamation. Nothing else can explain the spontaneous joy of the
primitive church, the dramatic transformation of the apostolic
band from an attitude of wistful disillusionment and cringing
cowardice into that of men whom no persecution could
silence, or the triumphant faith of their witness to a crucified
felon as the risen Lord of life.[5] As Bornkamm puts it, 'they
saw Jesus not as a mere figure of the past who found his
tragic end on the cross but as the living Lord, present through
the power of his resurrection'; and they proclaimed him as
'the decisive, redemptive, ultimate act of God for the world . . .
All titles of sovereignty which faith now assigns to him express
this fact: in him the turning-point of the ages has arrived, the
inauguration of salvation, and the nearness and presence of
God'.[6]

But the point I want to stress is this: the apostles made this
proclamation not as a beautiful myth,[7] but as something which
actually happened. The uniqueness of the Christian faith
consists in the fact that it was founded on a *unique historical
event*. It is true that 'empirical Christianity', like all other
religions, inevitably includes much that is false and unworthy
as well as a great deal that is noble and true. But it is distin-
guished from other religions by the event which gave it birth;
and it is itself continuously corrected and purified in so far as
Christians habitually go back to that event – and its necessary
implications – as their starting-point, their touchstone and
their inspiration.

This, then, will form the central theme of our present

[4] H. D. Lewis and R. L. Slater, *World Religions*, p. 195.
[5] Although we must, of course, add that it was only after Pentecost, and
their inner experience of the promised Spirit, that their transformation
was complete.
[6] *What can we know about Jesus?*, pp. 75, 82.
[7] *Pace* Bultmann and others. But I have discussed the evidence against
Bultmann's view, and the way in which some of his disciples are themselves
having second thoughts on this, in my recent book *Christianity: the Witness
of History* (Tyndale Press, 1969).

study: namely, the way in which this unique historical event distinguishes the Christian faith from all other religions. But this invites two obvious points of challenge: first, the historicity of this alleged event can be – and often has been – called in question; secondly, discussion must inevitably centre on how far it is really unique in its character and content. In terms of comparative religion the first of these points of challenge must emphasize the gulf between Christianity and those religions in which no real importance is given to historicity, while the second must focus on the essential differences between Christianity and even those religions which do claim a historical foundation – and, indeed, between Christianity and all other religions whatever.

First, then, the question of historicity; for there is all the difference in the world, as Lesslie Newbigin insists, 'between a statement about the nature of God, and a report that God has, at a certain time and place, acted in a certain way. In the latter case the occurrence is the essence of the message. The care which is taken in the New Testament to place the events recorded in the continuum of secular history is in striking contrast to the indifference which is generally shown with regard to the historicity of the events which Hindu piety loves to remember in connection with the character of the gods. There is no serious attempt to relate them to events in secular history, nor is it felt that there would be any advantage to be gained from trying to do so – even if it could be done. Their value is that they illustrate truths about God which would remain true even if these particular events had not happened.'[8]

This is not the place to discuss the vexed question of the vital connection between the Christ of the *kerygma* and the Jesus of history. It is true that liberal scholars have for years made the most strenuous attempts to get behind the apostolic proclamation of a divine Saviour with supernatural powers to a human Jesus who summoned men to the kingdom of God, who gave ethical teaching epitomized in the Sermon on the Mount, and who suffered the fate which threatens all those who fearlessly proclaim a message which their age and generation is not

[8] L. Newbigin, *The Finality of Christ*, pp. 52ff.

ready, or willing, to receive. But they soon found that this was a hopeless task, for it is impossible to eliminate the supernatural from the Gospel records without reducing them to a meaningless distortion. So, more recently, the pendulum has swung the other way – from the quest of the Jesus of history to an almost exclusive emphasis on the 'Christ of faith'. The Gospels, we are told (and this is patently true), do not provide the data for a detailed biography of Jesus, and make no attempt to give one. They were documents of faith, written no doubt with a theological intention which largely governed the writers' selection of the teaching and events which they record. But to recognize this is a very different thing from asserting that there is an unbridgeable gulf between the Christ of faith and the Jesus of history. It should, I think, be clear to the most casual reader that the Gospels profess to give us an account of the teaching which Jesus of Nazareth actually gave, the conflict with the religious leaders in which he was continually involved, the miracles which he in fact performed (and which so often constituted the starting-point of his teaching, or the *raison d'être* of official opposition), the way in which he was hounded – and voluntarily surrendered – to a criminal's death, and the triumphant sequel of an empty tomb and a risen Saviour. Even radical criticism, moreover, seems to substantiate most of the essential features of this picture beyond any reasonable doubt, as I have argued elsewhere.[9]

But it is not the details of the Gospel records with which we are, in this context, primarily concerned. So it will here suffice briefly to discuss, as evidence of the unique historical event which gave birth to the Christian faith, the summary of the apostolic tradition to which passing reference has already been made. In a letter which is indubitably Pauline, and which can be dated with virtual certainty in the middle of the fifth decade of the Christian era, the apostle states that he had already given to his readers by word of mouth (that is, *c.* AD 50) the tradition he was now committing to paper, and which he himself received as an authoritative tradition –

[9] See my book *Christianity: the Witness of History. Cf.* also Ferdinand Hahn, in *What can we know about Jesus?*, p. 45.

initially, in all probability, at the time of his conversion between AD 32 and 35, and in full detail, beyond any question, on his first visit to Jerusalem just three years later, about which he tells us in the first chapter of Galatians. So this takes the tradition right back to within some five years of the event.[1]

The tradition was this: that 'Christ died for our sins in accordance with the scriptures, that he was buried, and that he was raised on the third day in accordance with the scriptures'.[2] This, St Paul tells us,[3] was in no sense distinctively *his* message, but that of all the apostles; and he proceeds to substantiate it by a list of some of the principal witnesses to the resurrection – including the testimony of over five hundred persons who, he asserts, all saw the risen Christ on one and the same occasion and the majority of whom were still alive (to confirm or deny his statement) when he wrote.

Now it is perfectly true that some theologians are prepared to dispense with this unique event, despite the fact that it represents not only the central thesis in the New Testament but the very foundation of Christian faith down the centuries. Paul Tillich, for example, has committed himself to the statement that 'Religion cannot come to an end, and a particular religion will be lasting to the degree in which it negates itself as a religion. Thus Christianity will be a bearer of the religious answer as long as it breaks through its own particularity'.[4] On this H. D. Lewis – himself no fundamentalist – robustly comments: 'This is extremely wide of the mark. We do not begin to do justice to the Christian religion if we make the particular dispensable in the way implied in this passage . . . If a Christian does surrender the particular, in the way commended by Paul Tillich, he should announce himself boldly as a unitarian. If, as in the case of Tillich, it is not clear that he has faith in a personal God, he should make his home

[1] *Cf.* W. Pannenberg, *Jesus—God and Man* (SCM Press, 1968), p. 90.
[2] 1 Cor. 15:3, 4.
[3] 1 Cor. 15:11. *Pace* S. G. F. Brandon, *Man and his Destiny in the Great Religions* (Manchester University Press, 1962), pp. 195ff., who seems to ignore this verse completely.
[4] P. Tillich, *Christianity and the Encounter of the World Religions* (Columbia University Press, 1964), pp. 96f.

among the adherents of other faiths. Indeed, the proper place for Tillich and many of his followers today is in the Hindu religion. It is perfectly proper in that religion to teach that there is a point at which every religion "breaks through its particularity", that all our views are partial expressions of what altogether transcends them. But this is not a consistent course for a Christian. He can fully allow that there is much that is hidden from him . . . But at no stage does he hope to pass beyond the point where his experience derives its character increasingly from his realization of what God has done for him in Christ. Nor is there a divorce of the Jesus of history from the Christ of faith. The crucifixion did not mean, as some maintain, the total surrender of the Jesus of history to the Christ of faith. It was God suffering death in the form of a man, and this remains, for the Christian, the centre for ever of his life and hope.'[5]

We shall have to return to Hinduism again and again, but it is appropriate at this point, I think, to turn to those mystery religions with which Christianity has so often been compared. They were current in the very time and milieu in which the Christian faith itself had its origin; and it has often been suggested that it was from the belief that some of them included in a god who died and rose again that the early Christians postulated the unique event which constitutes the essence of the apostolic proclamation.

That there *are* parallels between the Mysteries and Christianity has been observed, as Bruce M. Metzger tells us, 'since the early centuries of the Church, when both Christian and non-Christian alike commented upon certain similarities'.[6] But he goes on to say that a number of the supposed parallels result from an arbitrary amalgamation of heterogeneous elements drawn from a number of different religions, and he quotes Schweitzer's statement that 'Almost all the popular writings fall into this kind of inaccuracy. They manufacture out of the various fragments of information a kind of universal Mystery-religion which never actually existed, least of all

[5] H. D. Lewis and R. L. Slater, *World Religions*, pp. 195f.
[6] B. M. Metzger, 'Mystery religions and early Christianity', in *Historical and Literary Studies* (E. J. Brill, Leiden, 1968), p. 6.

in Paul's day.'[7] He also quotes Edwyn R. Bevan's caustic comment: 'Of course if one writes an imaginary description of the Orphic mysteries, as Loisy, for instance, does, filling in the large gaps in the picture left by our data from the Christian eucharist, one produces something very impressive. On this plan, you first put in the Christian elements, and then are staggered to find them there.'[8] So the student of comparative religion must be on continual guard against what has been called 'parallels made plausible by selective description'.

Nor is it only the critic who may insert Christian elements in some of the mystery religions. In point of fact it is just as likely that Christianity influenced the Mysteries as that they influenced Christianity. As Metzger again observes: 'In what T. R. Glover aptly called "the conflict of religions in the Early Roman Empire", it was to be expected that the hierophants of cults which were beginning to lose devotees to the growing Church should take steps to stem the tide.'[9] On the other hand it is too often overlooked that the New Testament was written almost exclusively by Palestinian Jews, whose 'strict monotheism and traditional intolerance of syncretism' would have militated strongly against any wholesale borrowing from pagan cults. S. H. Hooke emphasizes the 'immunity of the Jew to the influences of the Mystery-cults' and insists that 'between the eternal, immortal, invisible, and only wise God, and the dying and rising gods of the Mystery-cults, there was a great gulf fixed'. So he considers it deeply significant 'that the first Christian community was wholly Jewish, and that the first great original Christian thinker was a Jew'.[1]

But the basic difference between Christianity and the Mysteries is the historical basis of the one and the mythological character of the others. The deities of the Mysteries were no more than 'nebulous figures of an imaginary past', while the Christ whom the apostolic *kerygma* proclaimed had lived and

[7] Quoted by Metzger, *op. cit.*, p. 9, from A. Schweitzer, *Paul and his Interpreters* (Macmillan, 1912), pp. 192f.
[8] E. R. Bevan, *The History of Christianity in the Light of Modern Knowledge* (Butterworth, 1929), p. 105.   [9] B. M. Metzger, *op. cit.*, p. 11.
[1] 'Christianity and the Mystery Religions', in *Judaism and Christianity*, Vol. I *The Age of Transition*, edited by W. O. E. Oesterley (Sheldon Press, 1937), pp. 237ff.

died only a very few years before the first New Testament documents were written. Even when the apostle Paul wrote his first letter to the Corinthians the majority of some five hundred witnesses to the resurrection were still alive, as we have already seen; and there must have been far more than this who could still testify from their personal experience to his teaching, his personality and his healing touch.

As for the motif of a dying and rising saviour-god, which has so often been compared with the unique event which gave birth to Christianity, Metzger points out that the formal resemblance between them must not be allowed to obscure the great difference in content. In all the Mysteries which tell of a dying god, he dies 'by compulsion and not by choice, sometimes in bitterness and despair, never in a self-giving love'. There is a positive gulf between this and the Christ who asserted that no man could take his life from him, but that he laid it down of his own will;[2] the Johannine picture of the cross as the place where Jesus was 'glorified'; and the Christian celebration of the Passion as a victory over Satan, sin and death. Similarly, there is all the difference in the world between the rising or re-birth of a deity which symbolizes the coming of spring (and the re-awakening of nature) and the resurrection 'on the third day' of an historical person.

It is true that there are certain parallels to this interval between the crucifixion and the empty tomb, for the devotees of Attis commemorated his death on March 22 and his coming to life four days later; there is one account of the death of Osiris, Metzger tells us, which makes the finding and re-animation of his body two or three days after his death; and it has been suggested that Adonis, too, *may* have been depicted as returning to life three days after his demise. But it is significant that the evidence for the commemoration of the *Hilaria*, or the coming of Attis back to life, cannot be traced back beyond the latter part of the second century AD; and the resurrection of Christ on the third day can, as we have seen, be documented as part of the authoritative tradition of the apostolic church from well before the middle of the *first* century. As for Osiris, Metzger writes that 'after his consort

[2] *Cf.* Jn. 10:17f. and Mt. 26:53f.

Isis had sought and reassembled thirteen of the fourteen pieces into which his body had been dismembered by his wicked brother . . . , through the help of magic she was enabled to re-animate his corpse'.[3] The contrast between this and the testimony of the apostolic church to the resurrection of Jesus is palpable. In the case of Adonis, again, the only four witnesses that refer to his resurrection date from the second to the fourth century of the Christian era.[4] If borrowing there was by one religion from another, it seems clear which way it went. There is no evidence whatever, that I know of, that the mystery religions had any influence in Palestine in the third decade of the first century. And the difference between the mythological experiences of these nebulous figures and the crucifixion 'under Pontius Pilate' of one of whom eyewitnesses bore testimony to both his death and resurrection is again obvious.

C. S. Lewis has given a good deal of thought to this question,[5] and has suggested an explanation of both the similarities and the differences between Christianity and the Mysteries (or nature religions). I am tempted to summarize his argument in his own words, but this would involve too long a quotation.

In the Christian story, he says, God comes right down from the 'heights of absolute being' into time and space; down to humanity, down to the very foundations of the Nature he had himself created. But he 'goes down to come up again and bring the whole ruined world up with him'. In this descent and re-ascent 'everyone will recognise a familiar pattern: a thing written all over the world' – in vegetable life, in animal generation, even in our moral and emotional life. 'Death and re-birth – go down to go up' – this seems to be a basic principle.

This principle is supremely illustrated in the incarnation. But Lewis argues that the pattern can be found in nature precisely because it was first there in God. It is true that 'the very congruity of this doctrine with all our deepest insights into life and nature may itself make us pause'. Does it not seem to 'fit' so aptly that the suspicion may arise that the idea of the incarnation must have arisen from men seeing this

[3] B. M. Metzger, *op. cit.*, pp. 19, 20.   [4] *Ibid.*, p. 21.
[5] C. S. Lewis, *Miracles* (Geoffrey Bles, 1947), pp. 135ff.

pattern elsewhere, particularly in the annual death of vege-
tation? 'For there have, of course, been many religions in
which the annual drama (so important for the life of the
tribe) was almost admittedly the central theme, and the deity
– Adonis, Osiris, or another – almost undisguisedly a personifi-
cation of the corn, a "corn-king" who died and rose again
each year. Is not Christ simply another corn-king?'

Now this, he remarks, brings us to a fact which seems, at
first sight, very strange indeed. For there *is*, from one point
of view, something similar between Christ and Adonis and
Osiris – apart from the basic fact that they 'lived nobody
knows where or when, while He was executed by a Roman
magistrate we know in a year which can be roughly dated'.
But the puzzle is this: if Christianity is a religion of that kind,
then why is the whole idea so foreign to the New Testament?
Corn-religions were both popular and respectable; so why
should the analogy be deliberately concealed? If the answer is
because the first Christians were Jews, then this raises yet
another puzzle, and we must ask ourselves why 'the only
religion of a "dying God" which has actually survived and
risen to unexampled spiritual heights' sprang from such an
alien soil?

'The records, in fact, show us a Person', he insists, 'who
enacts the part of the Dying God, but whose thoughts and
words remain quite outside the circle of religious ideas to
which the Dying God belongs. The very thing which the
Nature-religions are all about seems to have really happened
once: but it happened in a circle where no trace of Nature-
religion was present.'

It is at this point that Lewis suggests a solution. He emphasizes that the God who 'came down', died and rose again in
Christ was none other than the God of the Old Testament – a
God who was, indeed, the glad Creator of wheat, wine and
oil, the God of all Nature – 'her inventor, maker, owner and
controller' – who constantly works in nature the annual
miracle of death and resurrection. And yet he is very different
from a Nature God, for he himself undergoes no change whatever. Once, and once only in history, he intervened drama-
tically and decisively in the world of men in the life, death

and resurrection of Jesus of Nazareth. So, instead of this decisive act being suggested to the imagination of Christians by the facts of nature, the reality is precisely the other way round: namely, that the annual death and resurrection in-wrought in nature by her Creator provide us with a dim and partial picture of that incarnation, death and resurrection which represent the focal point of the action of the same God in human history, which must have been in his mind from the beginning of creation, and in which alone man can find the ultimate answer to the meaning and destiny of human life – and even of nature itself.

But whatever view is taken of this argument, E. O. James insists that 'there is no valid comparison between the Synoptic story of Jesus of Nazareth and the mythological accounts of the mystery divinities of Eleusis, Thrace, Phrygia or Egypt . . . Similarly, the belief in the Resurrection of Christ is poles removed from the resuscitation of Osiris, Dionysius, or Attis in an annual ritual based on primitive conceptions of mummification, and the renewal of the new life in the spring. The resemblance between the Christian Easter and the Hilaria in the Attis mystery on March 25th is purely superficial, there being no real points of contact in the "cult-legends" of the two systems.'[6]

We find this same tendency to mythology rather than history in Hinduism. This is the oldest of all the living religions and, to me, the most baffling, for it is made up of so many strata, it includes such a welter of heterogeneous concepts, and it means so many different things to its vast number of devotees. We shall have to return to Hinduism frequently in the course of this study; but we are now concerned only with any parallel to – or contrast with – the unique historical event which constitutes the very foundation and essence of the Christian faith. And here the position is clear enough. 'It is no accident', Stephen Neill remarks, 'that there is no indi-genous tradition of history-writing in India. The Greeks, the Hebrews and the Muslims all had their understanding of history, and the sense that it was worth while to take trouble to record it. In India the whole genius of the people seems to

[6] E. O. James, *In the Fulness of Time* (SPCK, 1935), pp. 87f.

have been turned inwards to contemplation and the development of speculative thought . . . Traditionally the Hindu does
not attach great importance to the events that occur in the
three-dimensional world of space and time, or to the human
beings that take part in them . . . Thus the Hindu has in the
past been inclined to take pride in the fact that Hinduism is a
religion of pure ideas, and in this respect to contrast Christianity unfavourably with it as a religion that is dependent on
history.'[7] Lesslie Newbigin tells us that he has never forgotten
the astonishment with which a devout and learned teacher of
the Rāmakrishna Mission regarded him when he discovered
that the Bishop was prepared to rest his whole faith as a
Christian upon 'the substantial historical truth of the record
concerning Jesus in the New Testament'. To the Hindu it
'seemed axiomatic that such vital matters of religious truth
could not be allowed to depend upon the accidents of history.
If the truths which Jesus exemplified and taught are true, then
they are true always and everywhere, whether a person called
Jesus ever lived or not.'[8]

But for the Christian the 'truths which Jesus exemplified
and taught' cannot be separated from the historical facts. It
is not enough to postulate that the nature and character of
God are such as Jesus declared them to be; for it is pre-
eminently through what Jesus *was* and *did* that God's nature
and character stand revealed, and it is meaningless to speak
of the efficacy of his atoning death unless he did in fact die.
But it is true that, with the event, we also need the interpretation put on that event by the apostles.

No doubt God reveals himself continually, in one way or
another, at all times and in all places – had we only the eyes
to see. This is a question with which we must grapple later.
But this does not mean that there must have been successive
incarnations, and that all that was lacking was men like the
apostles to apprehend and interpret them. No, the Christian
faith, based on the apostolic testimony, is that God acted in
Jesus in a way which was unique, which was never to be

[7] S. C. Neill, *Christian Faith and Other Faiths* (Oxford University Press, 1961),
pp. 87ff.
[8] L. Newbigin, *The Finality of Christ*, p. 50.

repeated, and which constitutes the decisive point in human history.[9]

There are, therefore, a number of fundamental differences between the Christian doctrine of the incarnation and the Hindu belief in the ways in which the deity has appeared to men. First, the *avatārs*, or 'descents', in which Hindus believe – and which awaken in some of them, beyond question, a passionate devotion – for the most part[1] concern mythological rather than historical figures. A Hindu may, indeed, commit himself to an *avatār* without any conviction that such a being ever existed in history.[2] Secondly, those Hindus who believe in a personal God (whether Vishnu, Śiva or Kālī, the mother goddess) conceive of Vishnu as having 'descended' in a whole sequence of *avatārs*[3] – sometimes in the form of a fish, sometimes that of an animal, but usually that of a man. Many of these – Krishna, Rāma, *etc.* – are themselves worshipped as gods – to all intents and purposes – in popular Hinduism (as also are Vishnu, Śiva and Kālī, of course); but they are all regarded as different manifestations of the Supreme Being by more sophisticated persons. It is quite easy for a Hindu, therefore, to accept Christ as yet another incarnation of the deity – but, as Gandhi put it, not to give him a solitary or supreme throne. Thirdly, to the philosophical Hindu a belief in these incarnations represents a somewhat low level of spiritual perception; but he will concede that one who cannot 'apprehend the deity in itself, even in a personal form, may need the help of some human figure to which he may cling as the only means by which . . . the divine can penetrate his spirit'.[4] And fourthly, some of these incarnations of the deity are

---

[9] *Cf. ibid.*, p. 76. *Cf.* also N. Smart, *World Religions: a Dialogue* (SCM Press, 1960; Pelican Books, 1966), pp. 90ff.

[1] An exception to this may be found in those who accept Sri Rāmakrishna, a mystic reformer born in 1836, or Chaitanya, a revivalist worshipper of Vishnu born in 1845, as *avatārs*.

[2] *Cf.* E. L. Allen, *Christianity among the Religions*, p. 108. But again, there can be no doubt that the simple Hindu takes these *avatārs* literally.

[3] Many Hindus postulate that there will be ten in all, of which the tenth is still to come. Many, again, include the Buddha among them.

[4] *Cf.* S. C. Neill, *Christian Faith and Other Faiths*, p. 83, summarizing the views of the late President Radhakrishnan. But others take quite a different view (see pp. 58, 64f. below).

depicted as falling very far short of what we should regard as moral perfection.

It seems unnecessary, therefore, to labour the contrast between these *avatārs* and the incarnation as Christians know it. Suffice it to say that it has always been emphasized that this was an historical event; that it was once for all, unrepeatable and 'without parallel or substitute';[5] and that it concerned the one who was not only the 'Father's only Son' but was also morally perfect, 'full of grace and truth'.[6] This finds a very early expression in the words of St Paul in his first letter to the Corinthians: 'Of course, as you say, "a false god has no existence in the real world. There is no god but one." For indeed, if there be so-called gods, whether in heaven or on earth – as indeed there are many "gods" and many "lords" – yet for us there is one God, the Father, from whom all being comes, towards whom we move; and there is one Lord, Jesus Christ, through whom all things came to be, and we through him.'[7] In these two verses St Paul is, I think, making three distinct points: first, that the so-called gods of the heathen do not really exist, and that an idol, as such, is 'nothing';[8] secondly, that there are, none the less – behind and beside these false gods – demons and other supernatural beings sometimes called 'gods' or 'lords' even in the Bible,[9] but they are in fact created beings; and thirdly, that there is only one true God, our Father, *by* whom all were created, and one Lord, Jesus Christ, *through* whom (as the eternal Word of God) all were created, and by whom we have been redeemed.[1]

Shintoism, the Way of the Gods, is the national religion of Japan. It has no systematic doctrine and no philosophy of its own, and seems to combine features of primitive nature worship with Emperor worship, while its moral teaching owes much today to Confucianism and something to Buddhism.[2]

---

[5] *Cf.* H. D. Lewis and R. L. Slater, *World Religions*, p. 193.

[6] Jn. 1:14, NEB.

[7] 1 Cor. 8:5, 6, NEB.

[8] *Cf.* 1 Cor. 10:19, 20.

[9] *Cf.* Dt. 10:17.

[1] *Cf.* Charles Hodge, *Commentary on I Corinthians* (Banner of Truth Trust, 1959), pp. 143ff.

[2] S. C. Woodward, in *The World's Religions*, 2nd ed. (IVF, 1951), pp. 136ff.

Sometimes the objects of veneration are mountains, islands, trees, rocks or waterfalls, which may or may not be connected with some legendary story or belief. Sometimes, again, the object of veneration is an animal-god or plant, or some mythological god or goddess. But none of this has any clear basis in history, – except, of course, the different Emperors of Japan. Much the same can be said of those primitive beliefs, all the world over, which are frequently subsumed under the title of Animism – of which primitive Shintoism was, indeed, the variety characteristic of Japan. Animism basically consists in the worship of, and endeavour to propitiate, those spirits which are believed to reside in natural objects such as trees, rocks or springs; but this is commonly combined with the veneration of the dead (who are regarded, together with the living and those still unborn, as constituting the mystical entity of the tribe or family), and sometimes with fetishism, totemism, taboos and magical practices of various sorts. But with Animism we virtually come back to those beliefs in a 'corn-king' and other features of nature religions which we have discussed already. Neither in Shintoism nor in Animism is there anything remotely comparable, therefore, with the unique historical event which was both the origin and the substance of the *kerygma* of the apostolic church.

Even in Zoroastrianism elements of nature-religion survive, together with much mythology. But with Zoroastrianism we pass over to those religions whose founder was certainly a historical figure; and although there is some doubt as to when precisely Zarathustra (or Zoroaster) lived, it seems probable that he was a near contemporary of Lao-tze (the founder of Taoism)[3] and Confucius in China, of Gautama the Buddha and Mahāvīra (the founder of Jainism) in India, and of Jeremiah and Ezekiel in Israel. The possibility of some cross-fertilization of ideas, therefore, can by no means be discounted.

In Taoism and Confucianism we find religions which might equally well be described as philosophies; and this may well

[3] Although there is considerable doubt about the date which should be assigned to Lao-tze, and it has even been questioned as to whether he was in fact historical.

be true of Buddhism too in its original form.[4] But at a later date Lao-tze came to be venerated as one who was carried in his mother's womb for seventy or eighty years and then born (scarcely surprisingly!) when already mature. Many Buddhists, moreover, have not been content simply to follow the teachings of the Buddha but have come to regard him as an incarnation of the deity in whom he himself may never have believed, and on whom, in any case, he put singularly little emphasis. A section of them also hold that he has been succeeded by an unbroken sequence of 'living Buddhas' by a special form of metempsychosis, or the transmigration of the soul of one such Buddha or Lama, when he dies, to another.

The outstanding 'historical event' in Buddhism is undoubtedly the vivid conviction of the transience of all things, and the mystery of suffering, which impelled Gautama to forsake the luxurious life of a young Kshatriya prince, and even his sleeping wife and infant son, first for the traditional discipline of the ascetic life and then for solitary meditation – followed, in due course, by his 'Enlightenment'. Far from keeping his new-found knowledge to himself, moreover, he set out on a wandering ministry to teach others how they, too, could escape from the bondage of desire. We shall have to come back repeatedly to the meaning and content of this experience of the Buddha, and to subsequent developments in the religion he founded – for Buddhism (in some of its forms) is probably the most attractive of all the non-Christian religions to the Western mind. But it will suffice, in the present context, again to affirm that there is nothing in Buddhism which provides any sort of parallel to that act of God – in the life, death and resurrection of Jesus – which transformed the apostles from ineffective cowards to triumphant witnesses and has constituted the essence of the Christian faith ever since. 'The peculiar significance ascribed by Christians to certain historical events has no place in Buddhism', H. D. Lewis asserts, 'and Buddha himself, according to the famous text which described his decease, disavowed at the time of his death any peculiar

---

[4] Although this has recently been called in question, and there is today profound agnosticism about the nature of early Buddhism. *Cf.* E. G. Parrinder, *An Introduction to Asian Religions*, p. 70.

claims to be made on his behalf as the instrument of salvation.
It was the doctrine that he bequeathed to others and it was
the doctrine that really mattered, although this advice was
extensively disregarded . . . There is certainly no once for
all redeeming event whose significance is to be preserved at
all cost.'[5]

In Islam we come to a religion which is not only clearly
historical but also rigidly monotheistic. We shall have to
consider its teachings about salvation and revelation in subsequent chapters; but the relevant point in the present context is that to the Muslim the one unforgivable sin is that of
shirk, or associating anyone or anything with the Almighty.
The very idea of an incarnation of the deity is therefore
anathema, or simple blasphemy, to the orthodox or Sunnī
Muslim (and the Sunnīs represent some ninety per cent of the
450 million or so contemporary Muslims). To them Muham-
mad was God's inspired prophet, and they have come to
regard him as impeccable and infallible, but not in any sense
divine. It is partly for this reason that they commonly object
to being called 'Muhammadans', since they think this term
implies that they regard Muḥammad in much the same way
as Christians regard Christ. To the Muslim it is the divine
revelation of which Muḥammad was the mouthpiece, rather
than any historical event, which is all important.

But as in so many religions, it was not long before differences
of opinion and multiplication of sects began to appear in
Islam too. It was during the first century of the Muslim era
that the Shīʿa, or 'sect' of ʿAlī, broke away – in some sense,
at least – from the main body of orthodox Islam. In due
course the Shīʿa itself split up into a number of conflicting
sects; but they were almost all united in the belief that God
could not have left the leadership of the Muslim community
to the vagaries of human election, but must himself have
designated a leader and have given him – whether directly
or through Muḥammad – esoteric teaching about the principles
of the faith. And who, other than ʿAlī (the nephew and son-
in-law of Muḥammad, a doughty warrior and an eloquent
orator), should this be?

[5] H. D. Lewis and R. L. Slater, *World Religions*, pp. 155f., 173.

The Shī'ī sects were also united in their belief that when 'Alī died he must have been succeeded by another Imām, or leader, who could continue to give authoritative teaching to the community. The splits between them were, in fact, almost all concerned with disputes about the succession to the Imamate. Most of them agreed that this was confined to the Prophet's grandchildren through 'Alī and Fāṭima, Muḥammad's only surviving child. Usually, moreover, the succession went from father to eldest son – and all the Shī'īs except the Zaydīs came to believe that the Imāms, like Muḥammad himself, were impeccable and infallible, and that a 'divine light-substance' which had been inherent in Muḥammad and other prophets passed from one Imām to his successor by a special form of metempsychosis.

The largest Shī'ī sect – the Twelvers (or Ithnā 'Asharīs) – believe that the twelfth of these Imāms withdrew, in 260 AH, and went into hiding in the will of God. In their belief he is, indeed, still alive, the sole medium of spiritual blessing, and he will one day reappear to bring in the golden age. The Ismā'īlīs, on the other hand, chose a different line of succession after the sixth Imām. At a later date they subdivided once again; and the twenty-first Imām recognized by one section, the Musta'līs, also went into hiding (although, unlike the Imām of the Twelvers, he is not regarded as still supernaturally alive, but as having been followed by an unknown number of successors), while the Imām of the other section, the Niẓārīs, is still present in the person of the Agha Khān – and is accorded, at least by the less sophisticated of his followers, almost divine honours. It can, indeed, be said that some of the Shī'īs have come to believe in what is very near to a principle of incarnation.

It is not altogether surprising, then, that further splits from the Shī'a have led to the founding of new religions. Such are the Druze, the Bābīs and the Bahā'īs. The Druze derive their name from al-Darazī, but their real leader was Ḥamza, who regarded the Fāṭimid Caliph al-Ḥākim as the 'embodiment of the ultimate One'[6] and the first cosmic principle. The Bābīs are named after Sayyid 'Alī Muḥammad of Shirāz, who

─────

[6] *Encyclopaedia of Islam*, article on *Durūz*.

was born in 1819 and was recognized as the 'gateway' (*bāb*) to truth, the initiator of a new prophetic cycle and the 'mirror of the breath of God'[7]; while the Bahā'īs are those who broke away from other followers of the Bāb in favour of Bahā' Allāh, one of the Bāb's first disciples, who declared himself to be 'He whom God shall Manifest'. As such, he certainly claimed to be a prophet in his own right, but he did not teach any doctrine of incarnation. Each of these three religions now has a theology and ethic of its own.

Bahā'ism, as we have already seen, represents a syncretic religion which combines elements drawn from several faiths in a novel synthesis. This is also true, in some measure, of the Ahmadiyya movement, although this has never wholly broken away from the body of Islam. Its founder, Ghulām Ahmad Khān, born in the Panjab about 1839, not only claimed to be the Mahdī (or 'Rightly-guided One') whom Muslims expect but also the fulfilment of numerous Messianic prophecies in the Old Testament and even an *avatār* of Krishna. One section of his followers regard him as a prophet in his own right, although 'within the revelation of Islam', while a more moderate section has resiled from this claim (which amounts to apostasy in the eyes of orthodox Muslims) and say that he was only a reformer (*mujaddid*).

But however this may be, what is crystal clear is that Islam as a whole makes no claim to any parallel to the unique historical event on which Christianity is founded; on the contrary, it would regard any such claim as blasphemous. To Muslims – even including the Shī'a – the Christian doctrine of the incarnation is *shirk*, for they think that Christians have put a mortal man, albeit a prophet who was virgin-born, on an equality with God. They find it desperately difficult to realize that in fact the movement, in Christianity, is not up but down: not exalting a man and equating him with God, but worshipping a God who became man. They also flatly deny that Jesus was ever crucified.[8] Instead, they believe that when the

[7] *Ibid.*, article on *Bāb*.
[8] Except, that is, for the Ahmadiyya, who have adopted Venturini's theory that Jesus was indeed crucified, but did not *die* on the cross. See my book *Christianity: the Witness of History*, pp. 62ff.

Jewish leaders came upon him with the intention of crucifying him, God could not allow this to happen to his chosen messenger, mere man though he was; so he caught him up to heaven to deliver him out of their hands, and then – by what we can only, I suppose, regard as a piece of divine deception – cast the likeness of Jesus on someone else, who was crucified by mistake in his place. So the unique historical event which Christians commemorate on Good Friday and Easter Day meets, from Muslims, an unequivocal denial, in spite of all the evidence to the contrary.

Finally, we come to Judaism – another historical and rigidly monotheistic religion. In Judaism Christians believe that God had in fact been preparing the way, down many centuries – by prophetic prediction and typological fore-shadowing – for the unique historical event which gave birth to their own faith. This, again, will engage our attention in subsequent chapters. But the majority of the Jews not only rejected their Messiah when he came but misunderstood those prophecies which had depicted him as more than mortal, which foretold his sufferings and death, and which accorded to that death a saving significance.

So we must end where we began – with the unique apostolic proclamation. This rests four-square on the atoning death and triumphant resurrection of the Jesus of history. To the Christian this event is absolutely basic. Its significance is reflected, as H. D. Lewis insists, in the radically different attitudes taken by Jesus and the Buddha respectively to the significance of their persons and what they came to do. 'When Buddha, at the time of his death, was asked how it would be best to remember him he simply urged his followers not to trouble themselves about such a question. It did not matter much whether they remembered him or not, the essential thing was the teaching – and what mattered about the teaching was the *Way*, to live so that at last, in this life or later, illumination and release would be ours too. It is almost, in this regard, like a scientific doctrine; it does not matter all that who pro-pounded it provided we can understand it and use it now. Its importance is in no way bound up with the way it was dis-covered. We can understand it without knowing anything of its inventor. But this is not the way of Christian truth.' This, on the contrary, is focused in the person of Jesus and in the historical fact of his death and resurrection; so we 'find that Jesus, the embodiment of self-denial and humility, also puts Himself at the centre of redeeming activity. He is Himself the way, the truth and the life, and his disciples, far from forgetting who He was or what He did Himself, are to come to Him, to be drawn to Him, and in sacramental worship to "Do this in remembrance of Me".'[9] It is deeply significant, moreover, that this remembrance was to be specifically in terms of his atoning death.

Other religions may, indeed, include the belief that God, or one of the gods, manifested himself once, or many times, in human form, or that some 'divine light-substance' has passed from one individual to a succession of others. But Christianity alone has dared to claim that 'the one, omnipresent, omniscient Ground of all existence' has uniquely intervened in his creation, not by assuming the mere form or appearance of a man, but by actually becoming incarnate; not by living and teaching alone, but by actually dying a felon's death 'for us men and for our salvation'; and by putting his seal on the fact and efficacy of this intervention by rising again from the dead.[1] This, in the apostolic proclamation, constituted the unique event which was the culmination of all that had gone before and the beginning of a new age. The Kingdom had come with power.[2]

[9] H. D. Lewis and R. L. Slater, *World Religions*, p. 174.
[1] See my *Christianity: the Witness of History*, pp. 38ff.
[2] *Cf.* E. O. James, *Christianity and Other Religions* (Hodder and Stoughton, 1968), pp. 66f., 166ff.

3 A UNIQUE SALVATION?

My last chapter was concerned with the *kerygma* with which the apostolic church burst upon the world, with its triumphant – and, indeed, irrepressible – proclamation that Jesus of Nazareth was not only the Jewish Messiah but a divine Saviour. We saw that the very foundation and substance of this proclamation was a unique event – the life, death and resurrection of a historical person; and that this was recorded at a time when a large number of those who had actually known him were still alive, many of whom could testify to a personal experience of having met the risen Christ.

It must now be our task to examine in much more detail the significance of this unique historical event as expounded by the apostolic church, first from the point of view of the new quality of life which characterized those who received the proclamation, and then that of the new insight into the nature and character of God to which it gave rise. In the first of these studies we shall be concerned with the Christian understanding of the purpose and goal of human existence, as compared with that of other religions and ideologies; and in the second we shall turn to the basic beliefs which lie behind all religions and ideologies regarding the reality, and nature, of the transcendental.

For my present subject I have chosen, after considerable hesitation, the title, 'A unique salvation?' I am aware, of course, that the word 'salvation' may seem somewhat traditional or even hackneyed; but I have chosen it because it seems to me more comprehensive than any of the other terms which might be used instead. It includes, according to the *Oxford English Dictionary*, both the 'state or fact of being saved', and the 'action of saving or delivering', so it will comprehend in its scope both what 'salvation' signifies in different religions and ideologies and also the means by which this salvation is achieved or received. It also properly covers both man's life here on earth and what may await him after life in this world, as we know it, has come to an end.

The basic meaning of the term, as I understand it, is that of deliverance or release. In terms of this life this means to be saved or delivered from injury, calamity, injustice, oppression, false attitudes, or sin; and in terms of the hereafter to deliverance from judgment, loss, separation from God or an endless cycle of re-incarnations. In essence, therefore, the word salvation means that a man is 'saved' or kept *from* something; but this necessarily leads, by implication at least, to the more positive concept that one delivered or preserved from sickness of body or soul is thereby made, or kept, healthy and 'whole', and that one saved from judgment after death, or set free from re-incarnation, is thereby admitted to future bliss – whether this is conceived in terms of 'heaven' or of release from individuality and the cessation of desire.

The first and most obvious distinction, then, is between those religions or ideologies which concentrate exclusively on this life; those which are concerned predominantly with the eternal world as they conceive this to be; and those which put a real – if not necessarily equal – emphasis on both. Another basic division is between those religions which teach that salvation must be achieved or realized, and those which emphasize that it can never be won but only received – together, of course, with how it is to be achieved or received, as the case may be. Another way of putting a similar, but by no means identical, distinction would be to divide religions into those characterized by law and those characterized by redemption. And whichever classification is used, this must necessarily involve a discussion of the widespread, but equally varied and even contradictory, concept of sacrifice or expiation found in so many different religions.

First, then, those religions and ideologies which postulate man's salvation – whether or not they would ever use that word – primarily or exclusively in terms of this world. Here

we think, first, of the great ideologies which are embraced
and followed today with quasi-religious devotion, and can
almost be termed 'political religions'. There can be little
doubt that some of the most dynamic forces in contemporary
society are to be found in movements which are primarily
political rather than religious, for Communism, Fascism and
various forms of Nationalism have shown themselves able to
move men's hearts, minds and wills to an extent that no purely
religious movement has done in recent years.[1] This is not to
suggest that these movements have influenced individuals
more profoundly or effectively than has religious conviction,
but rather that their power to evoke self-sacrifice and passionate
devotion has been more widespread. Indeed, these movements
possess, in Hendrick Kraemer's phrase, 'all the paraphernalia
of religion'. Thus Harold Laski described Stalin and his
associates as 'men who have a conviction that is religious
in its profundity. They have a "vision" of its character. They
are convinced that it is infinitely precious. They believe that
no sacrifices are too great for its attainment . . . They believe
that the only sin is weakness, that error is as profound a threat
to victory as was heresy to the Christian of an earlier age.
Their effort has for them all the elements of a crusade . . .
The Bolshevik, not less than the Puritan, is guided by his
Inner Light . . . The Bolshevik reliance upon their texts from
Marx and Lenin and Stalin is identical with the Puritan
dependence upon citations from the Scriptures.'[2] And the same
writer described the devotion of the German people to their
Führer in these terms: 'Worship of the Leader is made into a
cult. Hitler is the Chosen of God, omniscient, infallible, the
Father of his people, half ruler, half priest . . . His officials
express themselves as missionaries of a faith, the power of
which is beyond human ken. Its origin is wrapped in mystery,
it is not subject to the scrutiny of ordinary rational processes.'[3]
Similarly, in Nkrumah's Ghana, his title of 'Osagyefo' could be
(and no doubt was) interpreted as 'National Deliverer' by the

[1] Cf. E. C. Dewick, The Christian Attitude to Other Religions, p. 5.
[2] H. J. Laski, Reflections on the Revolution of our Time (George Allen and Unwin,
1943), pp. 71ff. quoted in E. C. Dewick, op. cit., p. 6.
[3] H. J. Laski, op. cit., p. 119.

more sophisticated, but was understood simply as 'Redeemer' by others; and I myself once heard choruses, which I had learnt as a boy to sing in praise of Christ, being chanted by Nkrumah's followers in his honour, with the minimum of verbal change.

In the case of Communism, this vision for which men are prepared to sacrifice everything is (with few exceptions) defined exclusively in terms of this life – to bring men, that is, deliverance from exploitation, poverty and social injustice and to substitute a new structure and ethos of society in which all men make their contribution to the common good without fear of want or the incentive of personal gain. It has almost always been coupled with an explicit atheism and a forthright denunciation of religion as the 'opiate of the people' which is exploited by the 'Establishment' to make the working classes content with miserable conditions here on earth in the hope of 'pie in the sky when they die'. And while it is true that both Mussolini and Hitler were not averse to invoking the name of God on occasion, as a hypocritical pandering to political convenience, it is clear that Fascism does not differ fundamentally from Communism in this regard.

Stephen Neill has pointed out that while Marx seems to have accepted the thesis of D. F. Strauss, that Christianity rested on a myth created by the suppressed Christian community of the decaying Roman Empire around the supposedly historical figure of Jesus of Nazareth, yet he was 'never able to escape from the world of the Bible. His own thought seems all the time to move in the same realms as the hopes of the prophets of the Old Testament and the eschatological expectations of the writers of the New. There is a biblical drama in which God is the chief actor. The Marxist picture seems to be a secularized version of the same drama with the principal actor left out.' So in place of the Kingdom of God there is to be 'a kingdom of man, in which oppression will wither away and man, delivered from his alienation against himself, will live in peace with himself and his brother'. Nor will this kingdom ever be established by the gradual victory of justice over injustice, but only by the violent revolution of man rather than the decisive intervention of God. There is even 'a sinless victim, the proletariat, through whose sufferings the exploiters of the past have made themselves rich', but whose agony is to end in triumph – to take the place of the Jesus on whom the sins of others were laid but whose sufferings will usher in a new world in which he will be exalted.[4] And Leslie Lyall has shown how the parallels to biblical concepts have not ended with Marx himself, for we find in China today that the Communist emphasis on confession of errors, followed by brainwashing, take the place of Christian repentance and conversion.[5]

The basic fallacy in this is not the emphasis on the exploitation of the proletariat in the past – and still, in part, today. This is sad and sober fact; and Marx was right to insist that this must not only be recognized, but changed. The fallacy lies, rather, partly in the myth of the 'sinlessness' of the proletariat, and the illusion that, were exploitation by the upper classes brought to an end, then discord, crime and sin would disappear and the golden age would dawn; and partly in the materialistic philosophy which thinks that every problem has an economic solution. Man, the Christian insists, was made in the 'image and likeness' of God, so the essential value of the individual must never be debased to the position of a cog in a state machine. But man is now a fallen creature, in whom the image and likeness of God, while still present, has been grievously marred and distorted; so it is not only society which needs a change in its economic structure, but the individual who needs a radical spiritual transformation. And this is something the gospel of Marx cannot effect.

But an exclusive emphasis on this life is not confined to the 'political religions'. This was also characteristic of the Sadducees. Whether they were mainly a political or a religious party, a rural aristocracy or state officials,[6] they did not believe in angels, demons, the resurrection or life after death. Instead, they put all their emphasis on the Pentateuch; and they taught that obedience to the Law led to prosperity and blessings, and disobedience to adversity and loss, here on earth. And although the Pharisees took a very different attitude

[4] See S. C. Neill, *Christian Faith and Other Faiths*, pp. 154ff.

[5] L. Lyall, *Red Sky at Night* (Hodder and Stoughton, 1969), pp. 69f.

[6] *Cf.* article on 'Sadducees' in *The New Bible Dictionary* (Inter-Varsity Fellowship, 1962), p. 1124.

to the immortality of the soul, it is clear that the primary emphasis in the Old Testament itself is on this life rather than the hereafter.

Similarly, a primary concern with this present life is characteristic of Zen-Buddhism today, whether or not this was also true of Buddhism in its original form – which is now regarded as an open question. It was the misery of suffering which prompted Gautama to leave a life of ease and family happiness first for that of the contemporary discipline of the ascetic path and then for that of solitary contemplation; and it was his solution to the problem of suffering which represented the heart of his 'Enlightenment'. He perceived that 'the root cause of the universality of suffering (*dukkha*) was intense desire (*tanhā*) arising out of the will to live and the will to possess'.[7] By this insight he attained the state of passionless peace called Nirvāna. Then for the sake of suffering humanity he made the noble choice not to remain in this condition but to set out on a wandering ministry of instruction and to found a monastic order to perpetuate his teaching. But this teaching, to which we must return, must be viewed in the light of the orthodox Buddhist belief in a series of rebirths; and it is chiefly Zen-Buddhism (together with some forms of Hinduism) which insists that the end of the road can be reached in this life. The emphasis in Zen-Buddhism (which appeared in China in the sixth century, and has exercised widespread influence from the thirteenth) is on concentrated contemplation, or *dhyāna*, by which they hope to attain *satori*, or enlightenment. Zen-Buddhists give little place to logic, words or letters, and stress 'immediacy';[8] and they differ from teachers of the Theravāda[9] form of Buddhism (to which they are much closer than to the Mahāyāna variety) 'in positing an enlightenment or intuitive grasp of truth not only at the end of the Path, but here and now, as they persevere in the Path itself'.[1]

---

[7] E. O. James, *Christianity and Other Religions*, p. 78.

[8] They thus have much in common with many existentialists.

[9] This is the title they themselves much prefer to the more generally used title 'Hīnayāna'. A Theravādin is one who follows the 'Doctrine of the Elders'; while Hīnayāna means the 'Lesser Vehicle', in contrast to Mahāyāna, which means the 'Great Vehicle'.

[1] H. D. Lewis and R. L. Slater, *World Religions*, p. 76.

Next we turn to those religions which put a predominant emphasis not on this life but on what lies beyond our present life span. And here we must give pride of place to Hinduism. To one school of Hinduism 'salvation' is essentially emancipation (*moksha*) from the bonds of this present existence and the material universe, all of which is regarded as *māyā* or illusion from the point of view of one who has attained his goal. It may even be said that the great theme of nearly all schools of Hindu thought is: 'Turn where we will, nothing in present existence is permanent. The Wheel of Life revolves, with sentient beings passing from one existence to another, be it as men or as gods or animals, be it on this earth or elsewhere, in the migratory *saṃsāra* process. Nor is this by chance. What is reaped is what has been sown. What has been enacted in some distant past affects what is possible in the present, according to the law of *karma*.'[2] The all-important goal is a changeless condition of 'peace and rest', for to the Hindu 'salvation' means *moksha*, and '*moksha*, as usually understood, means salvation or liberation not from moral guilt but from the human condition as such – it is liberation from space and time, and the felt experience of immortality'.[3] Different strands of Hindu teaching prescribe a variety of ways in which this union can be attained; and to these, again, we must return later. But it is fundamental to the Advaita Vedānta school of Hindu thought that there is in fact only one Absolute Reality (Brahman), so the union of the individual soul with the Universal Soul is already a fact, and all that is needed is to come to a full realization of this. The Sāmkhya-Yoga system, on the other hand, regards *moksha* not as 'seeing all things in the self and the self in all things', or the identity of the individual soul with the Supreme Soul (whose very existence it in fact denies), but as its total isolation from the whole samsaric world and all other 'selves' within its own eternal and timeless existence.[4] Such men as Rāmānuja, Namm'alvar, Tukārām and other *bhakti* teachers, yet again, take the view that release is only a prelude to a positive experience of union and loving communion with God.[5]

[2] *Ibid.*, p. 61.   [3] R. C. Zaehner, *Hinduism*. 2nd. ed. (Oxford University Press, 1966), p. 138.   [4] *Cf. ibid.*, p. 70.   [5] *Ibid.*, pp. 98, 128, 143f.

Much of this is not very different from the ordinary Buddhist view – which is not altogether surprising, seeing that both Buddhism and Jainism sprang from a Hindu soil. By contrast with Zen-Buddhism, it is orthodox Buddhist teaching that Nirvāna may normally be reached only after an indefinite number of rebirths. But this is a doctrine which is much more difficult to understand in Buddhism than in Hinduism, for Buddhists (unlike Hindus) deny that there is any eternal soul to be re-incarnated. What they believe is that desire (tanhā), if not eliminated, generates another being which inherits the karma of the person who has died.[6] All the same, it is possible in certain states of mind to remember one's former existences. Another fundamental difference between Hinduism and Buddhism is in the way in which liberation from these continuous re-incarnations may be sought and attained.

In the West, the Buddhist Nirvāna has sometimes been equated with annihilation; but this has been challenged by Buddhists themselves. What is extinguished, they insist, is 'not life itself but the craving and vain attachments which indeed must be destroyed if nirvana, the goal of Buddhist aspiration, is to be attained'.[7] Where Nirvāna is reached in this life, this is understandable enough; but where it is achieved only after death, the Buddha himself seems to have been deliberately vague about what is involved. Nirvāna has sometimes been described as 'the further shore, the harbour of refuge, the cool cave, the matchless island, the holy city. It is sheer bliss'. It is somewhat difficult, it is true, to see how a Buddhist who has reached a state of no-self (an-attā) can enjoy such bliss; and this seems to preclude comparison with 'doctrines of immortality found elsewhere, though not perhaps with some other interpretations of eternal life which are not so wedded to the conception of an imperishable, inherently immortal soul'.[8] But however this may be, the primary emphasis on life beyond the grave is unmistakable. This is also true of Mahāyāna Buddhism, however much it differs from the Theravāda

[6] Charles Eliot, *Hinduism and Buddhism* (Edward Arnold, 1921), Vol. I, pp. 191–198.
[7] H. D. Lewis and R. L. Slater, *op. cit.*, p. 63.
[8] *Ibid.*, pp. 63f. *Cf.* also N. Smart, *World Religions: a Dialogue*, pp. 51f.

doctrines in other respects. And it is still more obvious in 'Pure Land Buddhism'.

This brings us to those religions which envisage the life beyond, not in terms of Nirvāna or absorption in the Ultimate, but in terms of the entrance of the individual human soul into a fuller life beyond the grave – divided, it may be, into 'heaven' and 'hell' or their equivalents. Pure Land Buddhists depict the goal of their desire as a place where there are 'trees of gold, silver, lapis lazuli, crystal and coral'. But this is not to be interpreted in terms of sensual delight, for 'that Buddha's country is pure and peaceful . . . It is like the Uncreate and is like Nirvāna itself'.[9] In a very early text it is, indeed, regarded as a paradise whose inhabitants live in unbroken happiness until they obtain Nirvāna; but in popular esteem it is virtually equivalent to heaven.[1]

The description of the 'Pure Land' quoted above is reminiscent, in part, of the word-pictures of Paradise given in the Qur'ān and even of the Heavenly City in the Book of Revelation. There have, moreover, been both Muslims and Christians who have regarded life here on earth as of very little importance, and the attainment of Paradise or Heaven as the only matter of any real significance. Such were those Muslims who positively welcomed death in the Holy War, and those Christians who actively sought martyrdom. But the central strand of Christian and Muslim – as also of Zoroastrian – teaching is much more balanced, and regards both life on earth and life beyond the grave as of real, if not equal, importance. So it is to this view of 'salvation' which we must now turn.

Zoroastrianism puts a major emphasis on the importance of both ceremonial and moral purity in this world in the light of the judgment of the world to come, with its punishment for the wicked and reward for the righteous. Immortality is a constant theme in the Zoroastrian scriptures, together with the narrow Chinvat bridge which separates the good from the evil; and heaven is the reward for righteousness, while hell is described as an 'age-long and lonely misery of punishment for liars'.[2] In Islam, too, a primary place is always given to the

[9] *Ibid.*, p. 80.   [1] Charles Eliot, *op cit.*, Vol. II, pp. 29–31.
[2] R. E. Hume, *The World's Living Religions*. Revised ed. (T. and T. Clark,

sacred law, the Sharī'a, which prescribes in the utmost detail
those divine commands and prohibitions which constitute the
authoritative blue-print for the life of the individual Muslim –
and, indeed, the Islamic State – here on earth; but this is
invariably given in the context of the Day of Judgment, which
will bring the ultimate sanction for every transgression and
omission.

This dual emphasis on this world and the next is also, of
course, characteristic of New Testament Christianity. Christian
doctrine can never be exclusively concerned with the trans-
cendent world in view of the fact that when the eternal Word
'was made flesh' God himself became 'very man'. Jesus
taught, moreover, that men and women can be 'born again',
or 'born from above', here in this world; so eternal life for
the Christian begins here and now – although it will certainly
become fuller and richer in the world to come. Christianity
too, like Islam, believes in the 'resurrection of the body'; but
whereas the Qur'ān seems to depict this in starkly physical
terms, the New Testament teaches that the dead will rise
again not as mere disembodied spirits, on the one hand, nor
with physical bodies, on the other, but with new 'spiritual
bodies'.[3] And while this life lasts the Christian is required to
act as the salt and the light of the community in which he
lives, to fulfil all a citizen's duties, to love his neighbour as
himself, and yet to remember that his true citizenship is in
heaven, where his 'treasure' should always be. So Christianity,
as Michael Ramsey has put it, is intensely other-worldly
and at the same time thoroughly down to earth, requiring a
dual allegiance to the sacred and the secular.[4]

The Christian concept of salvation, moreover, is not restricted
to what happens to the individual soul after death. The New
Testament picture of the meaning of salvation includes what
Lesslie Newbigin calls 'the great corporate and cosmic com-
pletion of God's work in Christ, whereby all things will be restored to the unity for which they were created ... and God will

---

1959), p. 216.
[3] *Cf.* articles on *ba'th* and *ḳiyāma* in *Encyclopaedia of Islam*; and 1 Cor. 15:
35–54.
[4] *Cf.* A. M. Ramsey, *Sacred and Secular* (Longmans, Green, 1965).

be all in all. In that final consummation the whole history of the world, as well as the history of each human soul, will find its true end. To be saved is to participate – in foretaste now and in fulness at the end – in this final victory of Christ. According to the New Testament, the coming of Christ, his dying and rising and ascension, is the decisive moment in God's plan of salvation, presenting to every man who hears of it the opportunity and the necessity for faith, repentance, conversion and commitment to participation in the work of God in this present age.' To refuse this opportunity and thereby to forgo the possibility of salvation is to be 'lost'.[5]

But this necessarily brings us to the second part of our present study; how 'salvation' is attained. In some religions it must be achieved, won or realized by the one who is to be 'saved', whether by the quality of his life, the fidelity of his religious observances, or the merit of the sacrifices he offers. In others this salvation can never be earned by man, but can come only from a saviour-god.

In primitive religion there is always, I think, a recognition of a High or Creator God, as we shall see in our next chapter; but man is much more intimately concerned with a multitude of far more immanent spirits – good and bad, beneficent and malignant. These may, or may not, be identified with the souls of the dead. In primitive tribes there is little apprehension of 'good' and 'evil' as abstract ethical standards, but there is a vivid sense of the individual's participation in the life of his tribe or family – including, as we have already noted, both the dead and the still unborn. A man's primary duty is to preserve and strengthen the 'vital force' of his tribe, for on this its happiness and prosperity depends, and to take all necessary steps to ward off the loss or diminution of vital force which would result from any infringement of the rules and taboos by which tribal life is hedged about. If he fails to take such steps the retribution will be terrible. As a result, primitive religions are, above all, characterized by fear. Rituals must be performed to ward off the evil influence of those souls of the dead and other spirits which are regarded as dangerous, and to conserve the vital force of those ancestors

[5] L. Newbigin, *The Finality of Christ*, pp. 6of.

whose influence is benign. And the dependence of the living on the dead is matched by that of the dead on the living.[6] So the gifts, sacrifices and libations so characteristic of primitive religions – including, in some cases, even human sacrifice – are regarded as absolutely necessary to ward off evil and calamity and to preserve the life-force of both the living and the dead; and in this preservation lies their conception of 'salvation'.

When we turn to Hinduism we find a much higher and more sophisticated realm of ideas. Starting with the comparatively simple doctrine of the Veda, *yajña* (sacrifice) and *karma* (religious rites, or action in general terms) are regarded as the means by which 'salvation'[7] is attained. This becomes, in the understanding of a recent Hindu writer, the concept that 'life is a continual transaction between the gods and men in which man offers ceremonial gifts to the gods from the gifts they have bestowed on him and in return is enriched, protected, fostered. . . . Even salvation, even the highest good is to be gained by ceremonial sacrifice'.[8] But in the much more highly developed doctrine of the Upanishads and the Gītā release from space, time and the ever-repeated re-incarnations which the *karma*, or actions (whether good or bad), of the past and present inevitably entail, can be achieved only in one of several different ways: by fulfilling not only the temporal *dharma*, or duty, of one's caste but the eternal *dharma* which is still more fundamental; by practising the rigorous discipline of the Yoga technique and teaching; by coming to realize that individuality and all 'duality' is an illusion, and that there is in fact only One without any second, the 'One Brahman-Ātman which is Absolute Being, Consciousness and Bliss'; or by attaining, after liberation, to a state of unification – but *not* identification – with a personal God.[9] So salvation, to the Hindu, is attained – though very rarely, it would seem – by way of righteousness (or the eternal *dharma*); much more

---

[6] *Cf.* S. C. Neill, *Christian Faith and Other Faiths*, pp. 133ff.

[7] Both in terms of life here on earth and also of future bliss. *Cf.* Charles Eliot, *op. cit.*, Vol. I, p. 68.

[8] Sri Aurobindo, *Essays on the Gītā* (Aurobindo Library, Madras and New York, 1950), pp. 104f.

[9] *Cf.* R. C. Zaehner, *op. cit.*, pp. 96, 124, 70ff., 75ff. and 78f.

frequently by means of asceticism (*tapas*) and Yoga techniques; by knowledge (*jñāna*); or by way of devotion (*bhakti*). Any of these are means by which union with Brahman, however this may be defined, may ultimately be achieved.

Innumerable examples could be given of the earnestness with which many Hindus seek such salvation. But here a single illustration must suffice, as recorded by Klaus Klostermaier: 'We turned away from the river and came to an open stretch of land, a stony path between fields, hemmed in by low clay walls and thorny shrubs. It began to be hot. Every step kicked up dust. After a short while we came upon a young man, lying flat on the ground and apparently doing some gymnastic exercises. He got up, reached back with his left hand as far as he could, picked up a stone from a small heap lying there, stretched himself flat on the ground, reached with his right hand forward as far as possible and put the stone there on a similar small heap of stones . . . Dr. Govindam explained to me that the young man was not allowed to speak as long as he was occupied with this especially meritorious form of parikrama (circumambulation). On a particular spot of the parikrama route, 108 pebbles had to be collected and then moved, as shown by the young man, pebble by pebble, the length of the body at a time. After all 108 pebbles have been moved the distance of about two steps, one starts all over again. How long does it take to make the pilgrimage in this manner? Weeks – perhaps months. We passed other devout people who had chosen this penance, among them an old widow. Dr. Govindam explained to us that she was probably doing it to gain merit that would profit her husband in the other world . . . . Weeks later I saw her still at it, a few kilometres ahead of the spot where we had first discovered her. She seemed so weak that after every twenty metres she remained lying exhausted next to her small pile of stones.'[1]

Yet in Hinduism we also get glimpses of the concept of a saviour-god. This is particularly true of the picture of Krishna in the Gītā (which has come to dominate popular Hinduism), as may be illustrated by the story of how he several times

[1] K. Klostermaier, *Hindu and Christian in Vrindaban*, pp. 20f.

saved cowherds from a forest fire which had surrounded them on all sides and which threatened to suffocate them. But 'Krishna swallowed the fire, and thus man and beast were saved. The symbol of the forest fire is familiar to the Hindus as the image of the situation of man in this world . . . . The poor human being sees himself inescapably trapped. The miraculous intervention of Krishna saves him; only when God himself consumes the fire is man saved from being engulfed by it.'[2] According to this school of thought it is, indeed, through God's grace alone 'that the *karma* attaching to a soul can be cancelled out and that it can "become Brahman" and through becoming Brahman be in a fit state to draw near to God'.[3] This became the basic tenet of the developed *bhakti* movements.

We get the same double picture in Buddhism. Here too, as in Hinduism, the basic emphasis is on man working out his own salvation – as in the Theravāda doctrine and in Zen-Buddhism today. The way of salvation is by a knowledge of the Four Noble Truths: that existence necessarily involves suffering (*dukha*, or the 'mental and physical ill which is observed to accompany sentient existence as we know it here and now in contrast to the unspeakable bliss of nirvana'); that the source of suffering is our attachment to present existence, which amounts to a positive craving (*tanhā*); and that the only escape is first by resolving to have done with all such craving and attachment to the transient, and then by practising the eightfold discipline, moral and mental, of the 'Middle Way' – which is the path to Nirvāna.[4] But in the Mahāyāna form of Buddhism, which today is far the most widespread, we find a reappearance of the Hindu concept of *avatārs*, among whom Gautama was 'the latest and greatest of a series of eternal Buddhas who had appeared on earth to spread the saving Dharma[5] to suffering humanity'. There

[2] *Ibid.*, p. 23.   [3] R. C. Zaehner, *op. cit.*, p. 96.
[4] *Cf.* H. D. Lewis and R. L. Slater, *World Religions*, pp. 61f. Mention might also be made of the 'four sublime moods'; *cf.* A. L. Basham, *The Wonder that was India* (Sidgwick and Jackson, 1954), pp. 283f. See also Charles Eliot, *op. cit.*, Vol. I, pp. 213ff.
[5] Here meaning sacred law or principle of existence. In Pali the word is *dhamma*.

C

are also 'mythical heroes or Bodhisattva, who, following the example of Gautama, having attained perfect knowledge, refrained from entering upon the state of nirvana in order to help mankind by propagating the Dharma of the middle way. This magnanimous act involving the repetition of birth and death, and the pain and woes of mundane existence, was . . . comparable in its emotional appeal to that of the Gospel in Christianity in spite of the enlightened ones being actually mythical saints. Moreover, they did not sacrifice their own lives . . . as in the Christian doctrine of Atonement.'[6]

But even Mahāyāna Buddhism has developed in several different forms. Thus in Tibet it has fused with the Bon religion (itself, very probably, a mixture of primitive Tibetan religion with Taoism) to form Lamaism. This differs in many respects from Buddhism elsewhere; and one among several distinctive features is the way in which salvation is sometimes sought by the endless turning of a prayer-wheel.[7] In China and Japan, on the other hand, it has frequently taken the form of the Pure Land Buddhism to which reference has already been made. This looks back to a Bodhisattva[8] named Amitabha, who, long ago, 'accumulated such a vast store of merit during his progress towards Buddhahood that he vowed to bestow on all who trusted in him with perfect faith and sincerity, an assured rebirth in his paradise far away in the western quarter of the universe by the simple device of constantly repeating . . . "Hail Amida-Buddha" '.[9] This is expressed in the Shinshu teaching (which is the version of Buddhism most widely accepted in Japan today) in the hymn:

> 'Have ye faith in Amita's[1] Vow
> Which takes us in eternally.
> Because of Him, of his Great Grace
> The Light Superb will all be thine.'[2]

[6] *Cf.* E. O. James, *Christianity and Other Religions*, pp. 81f., although the idea of self-sacrifice is not foreign to Buddhist thought.
[7] *Cf.* Charles Eliot, *op. cit.*, Vol. III, pp. 394f.
[8] He is now a 'heavenly Buddha'. *Cf.* Charles Eliot, *op. cit.*, Vol. II, pp. 28–31.
[9] E. O. James, *op. cit.*, p. 83. The more usual spelling is Amita.
[1] Also spelt Amida. See above.
[2] H. D. Lewis and R. L. Slater, *op. cit.*, p. 78 – quoting *The Shinshu Seiten*:

In Zoroastrianism, too, there appears to be an expectation that 'before the end of the world, at intervals of a thousand years each, there will be three saviours . . . Each will be a supernatural descendant from Zoroaster'. Finally, the last of these, Soshyant, will with his assistants slaughter an ox, and from the fat of that ox 'prepare Hush, and give it to all men. And all men become immortal for ever'.[3]

The concept of a saviour-god was also widespread in Egypt and the Fertile Crescent. In Mesopotamia the dominant figure was the goddess Inanna-Ishtar, and her son-spouse, Dumuzi-Tammuz. Each year the young god died and had to be 'rescued and restored' from the land of the dead by Inanna-Ishtar, who resuscitated him and thereby revived life in nature and men. It was she, not he, who was the 'embodiment of creative power in its fullness' and the source of regeneration.[4] In Egypt, on the other hand, the saviour-god was Osiris, lord of the dead, helped and abetted by his sister-wife Isis. It was to Osiris that 'men turned more and more to escape corporeal corruption after death, and to attain a blissful immortality . . . . This, however, was accomplished by the correct performance of the prescribed ritual techniques whereby Osiris himself had been restored and reanimated by his devoted wife and sister . . . rather than by justification by faith in the saviour god.'[5] And while the appeal of the cult of Isis was primarily to women, it seems to have met the deeper needs of its initiates in a way that no other of the mystery religions did in the pagan world.[6] Yet it failed to make any permanent impression, as E. O. James emphasizes, 'because like the other cults it could not free itself from its underlying mythology. Behind it lay the long history of the religion of ancient Egypt whence it sprang, and though it spread rapidly and assumed increasing importance at the turn of the era,

---

the Holy Scriptures of Shinzu (The Honpa Hongwanji Mission of Hawaii, 1955), p. 236.
[3] *Cf.* R. E. Hume, *The World's Living Religions*, p. 217.
[4] E. O. James, *op. cit.*, p. 92.   [5] *Ibid.*, p. 89.
[6] The imaginative appeal of the Isis cult can be seen in Rider Haggard's series of novels which begins with *She*. The mythological elements are clear, and the novels make no claims whatever in the field of religious truth. They are a literary exploration in imagination.

despite its ethical and spiritual elements it could never get away from its ancestry and accretions.'[7] In other words, its fundamental weakness was that it rested on religious fantasy rather than historical fact; and this sharply distinguishes it from New Testament Christianity, and the unique historical event – totally unexpected, as it was, by the disciples – which gave birth to the apostolic *kerygma* with which it burst upon the world.

When we turn to orthodox Islam, we find ourselves confronted by a religion which sprang from a somewhat similar geographical area but differs from the mystery religions in almost every other respect. It has an unquestionably historical basis, and its central doctrine is a rigid monotheism. It is also pre-eminently a religion of law; and it would be easy to conclude that the attainment of salvation must depend on the quality of obedience to that law which characterizes the life of the individual concerned. But as in other matters, the Muslim community is divided in this respect into a number of different sects. In the view of the Khawārij (who are represented today by the Ibāḍīs of Oman and North Africa) anyone guilty of a major sin of which he has not repented ceases to be regarded as a believer at all. In the strict doctrine of the Shī'a, on the other hand, a Muslim who dies without recognizing the proper Imām 'dies the death of an unbeliever' – and many Shī'īs not only regard their Imāms as the sole media of divine blessing but attribute to the death of al-Ḥusayn at Karbala something approaching atoning significance. But the clear-cut barriers and distinctions between the different sects of Islam are now breaking down; and I think it would be fair to say that the great majority of Sunnī (or 'orthodox') Muslims, at least, today take the attitude that if they say the Muslim creed from their hearts, and if they make some attempt to fulfil their obligations in fast and prayer, they may have to taste the fire of judgment for a time but will eventually be 'saved' and admitted to Paradise by the timely intercession of their Prophet. The principle of sacrifice is by no means unknown, as the yearly festival of sacrifice (*al-aḍḥā*) testifies; but it holds no central position in the religion of Islam.

[7] E. O. James, *op. cit.*, p. 91.

In the Judaism of the Old Testament, on the other hand, the sacrificial system clearly held a central place, and the national Day of Atonement became the most important day in the year. But the sacrificial system, as James Atkinson puts it, 'operated increasingly as time went on by men with a deep awareness of sin, did not mean that by sacrifice a Jew hoped to attain God's grace, but rather that in penitence and faith he sought to retain it and avert its withdrawal. He sought in penitence to recover a favour, a relationship he had once known and had now lost owing to his sin; sin which would earn him wrath and death, if God were not gracious. The whole sacrificial system was an evangelical sacrament of forgiveness and deliverance, and forgiveness and deliverance were entirely God's work, never man's. It was not that man was doing anything to please or propitiate an enigmatic and uncommitted God who had not so far shown his hand. On the contrary, the central element in all Israelite worship was the collective liturgical recollection of all that God had done in their history in visiting and redeeming his people.'[8] But it is clear from the New Testament that legalistic Jews, instead of finding in the ceremonial law a way of forgiveness for their failure to keep the moral law, all too often put the two together and made out of them a method by which they tried to 'establish their own righteousness', instead of 'submitting to the righteousness' that only God can give.[9]

But the apostolic teaching about this vital matter was crystal clear. The 'blood of bulls and goats' could never atone for human sin,[1] and the value of the whole sacrificial system – ordained of God as the apostles clearly believed it to be – was twofold: first as an indication and a symbol of that repentance and faith without which, as the Old Testament prophets had passionately proclaimed, no religious observance was of any value whatever; and then as signposts pointing forward to the unique sacrifice of the 'Lamb of God' who was to come, of which all the sin-offerings and Passover lambs were mere foreshadowings. So the Old Testament sacrifices had to be

[8] James Atkinson, article on 'Salvation' in *A Dictionary of Christian Theology* (SCM Press, 1969).
[9] Rom. 10:3, 4.   [1] Heb. 10:4.

repeated 'year by year' – and even day by day – until in the
fullness of time they were 'done away' by the 'offering of the
body of Jesus Christ once for all'.[2] It was, indeed, to this
unique historical event that both type and prophecy in the
Old Testament scriptures – enacted symbol and verbal prediction – had looked forward, and from this event that the
Christian church had been born.

But this historical event was not only the fulfilment of the
sacrificial system, but also the basic essential of any fellowship
between a holy God and sinful men and women. Such fellowship was impossible without forgiveness; and a holy God, by
reason of his very nature, could forgive only on a moral basis.
It was not, as in so many religions, that man must try to
buy off the vengeance of a malignant God by the sacrifices –
animal, human or personal – which he must himself provide,
but that God so loved sinful man, and so longed to 'save'
him, that he had 'sent his Son to be the propitiation for our
sins'.[3] Nor was it that God had accepted the sacrifice of the
only man 'good enough to pay the price of sin', for that would
be unjust and unthinkable[4]; it was God himself – the God
who made us, who put us in this world, and who must have
known that we would fall into sin; the God who constitutes
the moral order of the universe, and cannot ignore sin; the
God who is the judge before whom we must all stand one
day – who was 'in Christ, reconciling the world to himself'.[5]

Thus in the apostolic *kerygma* this unique death, the efficacy
of which had been triumphantly vindicated by the resurrection, not only had a cosmic significance and effect, as we have
already seen, but provided the one and only basis for individual
forgiveness and salvation. To what this really means we must

---

[2] Heb. 10:10.   [3] 1 Jn. 4:10.

[4] *Cf.* Ezk. 14:14, 20, which shows that no man could ever act as a substitute
for another. Yet it is profoundly true that Jesus died also as our representa-
tive, and only a man can represent man. It was because Jesus was both
God and man that his death could be both substitutionary and represen-
tative.

[5] This reconciliation, as I have argued elsewhere, involves not only a
change in our attitude to God and sin, but also an objective atonement
which makes it possible for an ever-loving but always holy God righteously
to forgive the penitent sinner. See my book *Christianity: the Witness of History*,
pp. 79ff.

return later. In this chapter we must rest content with the observation that the basic emphasis that men and women must somehow work out their own salvation, which we find in so many religions – or achieve this salvation by the quality of their moral behaviour, their ritual observances or their religious devotion – seems to reflect the instinctive reaction of fallen man in rejecting any sense of need for supernatural grace. The ever recurrent motif of a saviour-god, on the other hand, may find its explanation either in terms of a primitive revelation, now largely forgotten, or of a conviction of personal inadequacy which represents the inner promptings of the divine Spirit – or, indeed, the ministry of that 'light that enlightens every man', however imperfectly understood.

4 A UNIQUE DISCLOSURE?

We took as our starting-point in this consideration of Christianity and comparative religion the proclamation, or *kerygma*, of the apostolic church, since this can be decisively authenticated from the pages of the New Testament. It found its origin and essence in a unique historical event – the life, death and resurrection of someone who had only just died, who had been well known to large numbers of people who were still alive, and whom many of them claimed to have seen after he had risen from the grave; for the *kerygma* had no other *raison d'être* and no other content. So our second chapter was devoted to a consideration of this phenomenon of the Christian faith in the light of the origin – whether historical or mythological – of other world religions.

Next, we began to examine in more detail the significance of this historical event as it was understood and proclaimed by the primitive church. Thus our last chapter was concerned with the way in which the apostles interpreted this event in terms of our human experience of 'salvation': that is, deliverance and liberation from evil, falsehood and sin in this life, and from judgment and misery in the life to come – and, indeed, the positive wholeness and confidence which this deliverance brought them, and which showed itself in the triumphant joy of the *kerygma*. It is now our task to examine the light this event shed for the apostolic church on the nature and character of God, and to compare her understanding of the Godhead, and of how he could be known to men, with that of other world religions.

There can be no doubt that the apostolic proclamation was firmly rooted in the revelation of God vouchsafed to Israel

in the Old Testament scriptures and in the history and
experience which lay behind them. In the Acts of the Apostles
Peter, Stephen and Paul all referred to 'the God of our
fathers'[1] and to the way in which he had revealed himself
to Abraham, Moses, David and others. Indeed, the apostolic
kerygma emphasizes the fundamental unity, the uncompromis-
ing holiness and the loving providence of the God who had
repeatedly intervened in human history, and who had not
only confronted the Old Testament characters in vivid
existential experience but who had actually spoken to them in
words which had been recorded.

It is also clear that they associated the Jesus of the New
Testament proclamation with the God of the Old Testament
revelation in a way wholly different from their attitude to
any other figure in their history. They had not yet, it is true,
worked out an articulated doctrine of the Trinity – a doctrine,
indeed, which could never have emerged from metaphysical
speculation but was forced upon them by the facts of personal
experience and the data of divine disclosure – but they
instinctively identified Jesus with Yahweh, freely applied to
him the divine names and attributes, and regarded him as the
very image and likeness of the invisible God. To this we shall
have to return in more detail later; but it must first be our
task to consider this understanding of the Godhead in the
light of the concepts and teachings of other religions.

Not so long ago many anthropologists were content confidently to describe the development of the religious thought
and understanding of mankind in terms of a simple progress,
or evolution. Starting from magic, man had first embraced
animism, then polytheism and then monotheism – from which,
of course, some would regard atheism as a further stage of
progress, when the age of religion which had displaced that of
magic itself gives place to that of science. But this thesis can
no longer be sustained. Religion can scarcely be said to have
arisen 'out of the failure of the magician to exercise his
functions properly', for in point of fact religion and magic
everywhere 'occur side by side and are inextricably inter-
woven'. Indeed, it is not only in preliterate states of culture

[1] Acts 3:13; 7:32; 22:14; *etc.*

that 'supreme beings, animistic spirits and animatistic conceptions of the sacred and numinous coincide with magical
devices, divination and soothsaying', but religion and magic
are also recurrent phenomena in predominantly scientific civi-
lizations. It is impossible therefore, E. O. James declares, 'to
maintain evolutionary sequences along the lines adopted by
Tylor, Frazer and their contemporaries'.[2]

There is, moreover, a great deal of evidence against the
assumption that the development of religion itself has always
been from polytheism to monotheism. In the contemporary
world, the study of primitive religions seems to have established
that everywhere – even among the most remote and primitive
tribes – there is a concept of one High or Supreme God. Thus
Stephen Neill insists that there can now be scarcely any doubt
about the existence of such a belief. 'There are', he says,
'still a few unexplored corners of the earth, and no doubt
there are still surprises awaiting the anthropologists and
others who interest themselves in simple peoples. But the
myth that affirmed the existence of tribes which have no
religion at all has steadily been exploded by the progress of
research; and some of the most striking evidences of a comparatively high level of religious understanding have been
obtained among the peoples which live on the lowest level of
subsistence and culture. Thus Fr. W. Schmidt (1868–1954),
who has given more elaborate study to this line of research
than any other scholar, found that among the pygmies of
Central Africa . . . there is a clear sense of the existence of
one Supreme Being to whom all other existences, natural or
supernatural, are subject.'[3]

But it is equally clear that this High or Supreme God is
given remarkably little thought, prominence or attention in
the rites and observances of most primitive religions. Instead,
men and women are absorbed by the need to propitiate a
multitude of far more immanent spirits. 'In many primitive
people', indeed, 'the High God appears to be regarded as a

[2] E. O. James, *Christianity and Other Religions*, p. 22.
[3] S. C. Neill, *Christian Faith and Other Faiths*, p. 131. *Cf.* W. Schmidt, *The Origin and Growth of Religion*, translated by H. J. Rose (Methuen, 1931), pp. 88, 191f., *etc.*

somewhat otiose and functionless being, who after creating the world wandered away into a far region, and so is now no longer very relevant to the practical affairs of life; he is not the object of a cult, nor is sacrifice offered to him.'[4] This does not seem to suggest that the followers of such religions are steadily pressing forward from a crude polytheism to a pure monotheism. On the contrary, it would seem to indicate that they have either abandoned in practice a monotheism they once knew and still vaguely remember, or that they are fighting against an inner conviction, dimly apprehended, which runs counter to their religious practice. Thus W. Schmidt himself regards the phenomena as evidence of the survival, in part, of a primitive revelation of God which has become obscured and overladen by magic, animism, polytheism and delusion.[5] The other interpretation suggested above – which may, indeed, be supplementary rather than contradictory to this – is given by the apostle Paul when he states, that men suppress or stifle the truth that they really know. 'For all that may be known of God by men lies plain before their eyes; indeed God himself has disclosed it to them. His invisible attributes, that is to say his everlasting power and deity, have been visible, ever since the world began, to the eye of reason, in the things he has made. There is therefore no possible defence for their conduct; knowing God, they have refused to honour him as God, or to render him thanks. Hence all their thinking has ended in futility, and their misguided minds are plunged in darkness. They boast of their wisdom, but they have made fools of themselves, exchanging the splendour of immortal God for an image shaped like mortal man, even for images like birds, beasts, and creeping things.'[6]

Nor is this true only of the primitive religions. Indeed, Schmidt and his collaborators have shown that a belief in some supreme being is of almost universal occurrence.[7] It can be found in ancient Egypt,[8] Mesopotamia,[9] Iran[1] and China,

[4] S. C. Neill, *op. cit.*, p. 132 – quoting A. C. Bouquet from C. R. Hopgood in *African Ideas of God*, edited by E. W. Smith (Edinburgh House Press, 1950), p. 69.
[5] W. Schmidt, *op. cit.*, p. 198.   [6] Rom. 1:19–23, NEB.
[7] W. Schmidt, *op. cit.*, pp. 251ff.   [8] *Cf.* E. O. James, *op. cit.*, p. 51.
[9] *Ibid.*, pp. 53, 54.   [1] *Ibid.*, pp. 60–62.

for example; but it has in each case been combined with, or overlaid by, polytheistic beliefs and practices. The possibility of some cross-fertilization of ideas between one religion and another cannot, of course, be excluded; but the evidence for retrogression in religious beliefs and practices in some cases seems to be at least as cogent and convincing as that put forward for progress. And if the import of the Old Testament is not to be distorted beyond recognition on the basis of pre-conceived ideas, it seems plain that the history of Israel constitutes a unique record of a primitive monotheism which was repeatedly compromised by man's fatal tendency to lapse into superstition, idolatry and unbelief – only to be recalled, temporarily, by yet another summons to return to the God he already knew but so easily forsook, and who never ceased to inspire one prophet after another with what may justly be termed an ever-deepening disclosure of himself.

When we turn to the religions which are extant in the world today we find the most bewildering variety of beliefs on this subject. Of the primitive religions little more need be said in this context; but even the most superficial study of Hinduism reveals that it is made up of many different strands and is understood by different people in very different ways. It can scarcely be denied that the popular Hinduism of the masses, for example, represents a form of polytheism (or, at best, a very qualified monotheism[2]) to which expression is given in a variety of idolatrous practices; but the same religion is interpreted by more sophisticated persons sometimes in panthe-istic, sometimes in monotheistic, and sometimes in monistic[3] terms. Buddhism, too, takes a number of different and even contradictory forms, and can be understood either as a theistic religion, as a variety of monism, or as a philosophy which puts a primary emphasis on man. In Zoroastrianism, again, we find an explicit dualism[4] which constitutes an alternative to either theism or monism in its approach to the problem of evil. But this problem is so intractable, and so basic to our

[2] More precisely, henotheism.
[3] Monism is the doctrine that denies all duality, and asserts that only one Reality, whether personal or impersonal, exists – and nothing else whatever.
[4] There is a valuable discussion of this in S. G. F. Brandon, *Man and his Destiny in the Great Religions*, pp. 258ff.

experience, that it will, I think, provide us with an illuminating approach to the way in which different religions have tried to explain the meaning of life and those principles or influences – divine, human or Satanic – which determine its course.

In a polytheistic religion this problem finds a comparatively simple solution. There are good gods and bad gods, benevolent gods and malignant gods, so all depends on which of these different deities is in control at any particular time or place. They are in continual, or at least intermittent, conflict, and neither one side nor the other is necessarily destined to prevail. And the picture is not very different when we turn to Hinduism in its popular form. But Hinduism as understood by more sophisticated persons can be interpreted, as we have seen, as a monotheistic religion, as a form of pantheism, or as an impersonal monism. Those who understand Hinduism as a monotheistic religion regard both good and evil as created by, and proceeding directly from, the same God. Thus Klaus Klostermaier, after watching an incident in which a goat died of sunstroke and was immediately torn to pieces first by vultures, then by dogs and finally by jackals, writes: 'God was the creator and preserver and destroyer. The reason for placing creatures in a desert, in a cruel world, in death – that was his caprice, his play, his lila. First he had created the sun who would one day kill the goat he had also created. He had created the vultures who would consume the goat. The dogs and jackals who would tear the skin to pieces and crack the bones with their teeth, they also were his creatures. *One* atman in all of them – in God and in the vulture, in the goat and in the dog. And also in the one who watched all this, trying to understand. God was the kind mother – and the bloodthirsty goddess of destruction. When misfortune goes on increasing, when catastrophe breaks all bounds, it is imperative to sacrifice to the goddess: her long tongue hangs bloodthirstily from her mouth, she holds a bloodstained sword, cut-off heads and arms are hanging decoratively over her naked breasts. Life issued from God's countenance – death from his back. God is the sacrificer and the sacrifice. Goat and vulture are his manifestations – adoration is due to both.'[5]

[5] K. Klostermaier, *Hindu and Christian in Vrindaban*, p. 46. It is only among

It seems clear that here a monotheistic and pantheistic interpretation of Hinduism come very close together. On the one view all that exists, whatever its moral character, proceeds directly from the same God; on the other all that exists constitutes, and is essentially one with, the deity. To those who hold to a rigidly monistic philosophy, again, there is only one Being – impersonal and absolute – and nothing else has any real existence. The visible world is basically regarded as illusion (*māyā*) and moral evil as ignorance, or at least as the fruit and evidence of ignorance. It is true that Hindus believe that unworthy behaviour leads to a re-incarnation lower down in the scale of life, and that a fulfilment of one's *dharma* or duty will result in a happier re-incarnation; but it is only by renunciation that the soul can achieve *moksha*, or release from both ignorance and transience. This is the final goal. And while the present life is predetermined by the past, the future depends on what man does in the present. It is, indeed, the final purpose of God – in the view of those Hindus who believe in a personal deity – ultimately to bring all souls to 'final liberation . . . from the trammels of matter which is itself his own "lower nature". He binds that he may loose and that he may lead all souls back to himself whether they like it or not. This is the eternal "game" that he plays with creation, but like any game it has its own rules, and the rules of the game are called *dharma*. God alone knows the rules, but he can and does on occasion reveal them to man as Krishna[6] did to Arjuna and man, in his turn, obeys the rules willy-nilly,[7] for he is conditioned by his own *karma* – the works that follow him from lives lived long ago into his present life with the same blind instinct that enables the calf to find the mother-cow wherever she may be in the herd . . . Arjuna may not

---

the Tamil-speaking Śaivites (*i.e. bhaktas*, or devotees of Śiva) that we find an intense sense of personal guilt from which a man can be saved only by the grace of God (in which we may, perhaps, see Christian influence); while Rāmānuja taught that God is 'possessed of all good qualities to a super-lative degree'. (See R. C. Zaehner, *Hinduism*, pp. 130, 132ff. and 99). In this context see also N. Smart, *World Religions: a Dialogue*, pp. 111ff.

[6] In one of Vishnu's incarnations, in which he instructs Arjuna, one of the warrior caste, about *dharma* and much else.

[7] This is, perhaps, somewhat of an overstatement. See above.

understand with his finite intellect why a fratricidal war involving the slaughter of millions is both necessary and right and therefore part and parcel of "eternal *dharma*" itself, but loath though he may be to take his cousins' lives he is not in fact a free agent, and must. However wrong the *dharma* imposed on you by your caste and by circumstances may appear to you, you are none the less in duty bound to do it.' The mythological story of Yudhishthira shows the distinction which some Hindus came to make, with much agony of soul, between the *dharma* of their caste, as interpreted by the Brahmans and even taught by the divine Krishna, and the eternal *dharma* which, in St Paul's words, is written on men's hearts.[8] It was the latter which Gandhi and other reformers have sought to follow.

It is, perhaps, fair to say that this is why there is, in general, little compassion in Hinduism and little effort to save men from suffering. It is all predestined, and if all is the outworking of an age-old chain of *karma*, then what duty – and what right – has man to interfere? It is this that lies at the root of the caste system, for it is here that the Hindu finds the explanation of every inequality and misfortune in life. Yet with that inherent contradiction which so often seems to characterize Hinduism, there remains the hope that by acquiring merit in this life a man may attain to a higher stage in his next existence, and ultimately to release from the endless wheel of existence and change.[9] It is quite clear, moreover, that a passive acceptance of suffering and injustice is not by any means the characteristic of many Hindus today. It was explicitly repudiated, for example, by S. Radhakrishnan when he wrote: 'Man is not at the mercy of inexorable fate. If he *wills*, he can improve on his past record. There is no inevitability in history. To assume that we are helpless creatures caught in the current which is sweeping us into the final abyss is to embrace a philosophy of despair, of nihilism.'[1] Stephen Neill has gone so far as to say that the 'heaviest blow at the traditional

---

[8] R. C. Zaehner, *Hinduism*. 2nd ed. (Oxford University Press, 1966), pp. 103, 115-124, *etc. Cf.* Rom. 2:15.

[9] *Cf.* S. C. Neill, *Christian Faith and Other Faiths*, pp. 72f.

[1] *Recovery of Faith* (1956), p. 4 – as quoted by Stephen Neill, *op. cit.*, p. 86.

doctrine of *karma* was dealt by Mr Gandhi, not by his teaching but by the manner of his death at the hand of an assassin. If all misfortune is the fruit of ancient deeds, then such a violent death should be evidence of a gravely sinful past . . . The death of Mr Gandhi . . . has challenged the Hindu with something he cannot interpret within the categories of his traditional thinking.'[2] But I doubt, with respect, whether a Hindu would in fact look at the matter in this way, for somewhat similar examples could be quoted from Hindu mythology.

Buddhism, as is well known, sprang from Hinduism. Gautama took over from Hinduism a belief in *karma* and taught that the 'cravings and lusts which are not overcome in this life leave behind them a *karma* which creates a new being. So the good and evil in our minds are the result of *karma*.'[3] The distinctive emphasis in Buddhism is on the suffering which is inherent in all sentient life, and for which the only cure – in the words of Stephen Neill – is to 'abolish the ego, which believes that it suffers, and there will no longer be anything that can suffer . . . The elimination of the self is the heart and the centre of all Buddhist philosophy.' More precisely, the idea of 'abolishing' the ego scarcely represents Buddhist thought, for what Buddhism actually teaches is that we must recognize that the ego does not really exist. There can be no doubt, however, that Gautama propounded a way of salvation which depended on man's own efforts and on nothing else. Thus all sin, to the Buddhist, is a manifestation of *tanhā* (craving or desire). Not that desire in itself is necessarily evil; it is desire for the pleasures of the material world, and either clinging to existence or craving for immortality, that is evil.[4] As a remedy for this, Buddhism puts a primary emphasis on right living – and on the purification of the heart from lust or craving – and the Buddha himself has always been regarded as an outstanding example not only of wisdom but also of virtue. In Buddhism in its Mahāyāna form, moreover, the belief in Bodhisattva, or Beings of Enlightenment who defer their own final deliverance from the world in order to save other people, 'implies the conviction that merit can be

---

[2] *Ibid.*, pp. 86f.   [3] E. G. Parrinder, *An Introduction to Asian Religions*, p. 71.
[4] *Cf.* S. C. Neill, *op. cit.*, p. 117.

transferred from one person to another'.[5] But this is, of course, contrary to the older conception of *karma*.

In Zoroastrianism, on the other hand, we find quite a different approach to the problem of evil. In this religion good and evil are set in the sharpest antithesis. It seems, moreover, that Zarathustra refashioned a Vedic polytheism into what was initially a clearly monotheistic religion, in which Ahura Mazda, the 'Wise Lord', was to be worshipped as the sole creator. But Zarathustra also recognized a fundamental dualism, with the followers of the Lie (the Druj, or Angra Mainyu) in conflict with the followers of Truth (Asham, or Spenta Mainyu). These two spirits, personifying darkness and light respectively, were regarded as having existed before the world was created and as implacably opposed to each other – each with his retinue of angels or demons, as well as his human followers. Originally, however, they seem to have been regarded as meeting in the higher unity of Ahura Mazda, who was 'holy, righteous and true, the greatest and best, wisest and most perfect supreme ruler and controller of all things.'[6] He was, however, the author of both good and evil; and this opened the way, in the later Mazdaean literature of the Sassanian period in the fourth century AD, for a clear-cut dualism, in which the Lie became Ahrimān, the Evil One, co-eval with Ormuzd (a combination of Ahura Mazda and Spenta Mainyu). These were regarded as two equally powerful forces of good and evil, locked in perpetual conflict – but with the good destined ultimately to prevail. In this whole context, however, we need to remember the historical relations between Persia and Israel, the distinct possibility that there was some contact between Zarathustra and contemporary Jewish prophets, and even the hypothesis that it was from Persia that the Magi came.

In Islam we come to a religion in which a rigid monotheism

---

[5] E. G. Parrinder, *op. cit.*, p. 102. This is also a matter of popular belief in India. It should, perhaps, be added that an exception to the high moral standards normally taught in Buddhism can be found in some of the practices of the 'Vehicle of the Thunderbolt' and in tantric forms of Buddhism. See A. L. Basham, *The Wonder that was India*, pp. 280ff.

[6] E. O. James, *Christianity and Other Religions*, p. 62. See also S. G. F. Brandon, *Man and his Destiny in the Great Religions*, pp. 258ff.

is the central doctrine. This was, no doubt, partly derived
from contact with Jews and Christians, but partly also from
some Arabian monotheists named Ḥanīfs. A belief in angels is
absolutely enjoined on the Muslim, and two Recording
Angels are believed to attend on every man – the one to record
his good deeds, and the other his misdeeds. The Devil (*Iblīs*
or *al-Shayṭān*) is regarded as either a fallen angel or *jinnī*[7]
who disobeyed God's command to do homage to Adam, and
is now the arch-tempter of mankind and the chief of a host of
evil spirits.

But while the teaching of Islam is far clearer and fuller
about the revelation of God's law for man than any disclosure
of his character and nature, it regards it as a much more
heinous sin to doubt or question that revealed law than to fail
to keep it. Indeed, in the strictest school of Islamic orthodoxy,
the Ash'ariyya, *everything* flows from the creative power of
God. It is true that God creates in his creature power (*qudra*)
and choice (*ikhtiyār*); but he then 'creates in him his action
corresponding to the power and choice thus created. So the
action of the creature is created by God as to initiative and as
to production; but it is *acquired* by the creature. By acquisition
(*kasb*) is meant that it corresponds to the creature's power and
choice, previously created in him, without his having had
the slightest effect on the action. He was only the *locus* or
subject of the action.'[8] It was in this way that al-Ash'arī
attempted to account for man's apparent power of choice and
moral responsibility; but it is clear that in reality it is God who
is the sole author of both good and evil. The Mu'tazilī heresy
had taught that God always acts in accordance with justice;
but al-Ash'arī would have none of this. Not only so, but in
the view of the Ash'ariyya God does not command the good
because it is inherently good, or forbid the evil because it is
essentially evil, but man's actions become good or evil simply
and solely because God commands the one and forbids the
other. All therefore proceeds from his will and decree – what

---

[7] *I.e.* genie. The angels were created from light, the *jinn* from fire, man
from clay.
[8] D. B. Macdonald, *Muslim Theology, Jurisprudence and Constitutional Theory*
(New York, 1903), p. 192.

is evil and what is good, and whether man embraces the one or the other. Yet at the end of time Iblīs is to be thrown into the fire of hell, together with his hosts and all the damned.

But this is not – by any means – the only strand of teaching in Islam. To the Muʿtazilīs passing reference has already been made; but there were also many mystics, or Ṣūfīs, who interpreted the Qur'ān in terms of Neoplatonism and also adopted a good deal of teaching derived from India. To them the one God became the One in an absolute sense; it was not only that there were no other gods, but that there was no other reality. This verged, to say the least, on pantheism or monism; but there is no doubt that many Ṣūfīs replaced the austerity of orthodox Islam with a passionate quest for, and devotion to, a personal God.

From all this it is obvious that the attitude of the different religions to the problem of evil gives us a vivid picture of the way in which they conceive of God himself. And exactly the same is true of the Old and New Testaments. It would be easy to comment in detail on the similarities and differences between Zoroastrian and Islamic teaching on this subject, on the one hand, and that of the Bible, on the other. In the Old Testament there is the same intense emphasis that we find in Islam on the unity and sovereignty of Yahweh; but there is also an emphatic insistence on his holiness. It is to this that both the sacrificial system and the impassioned teaching of the prophets bore witness. God is indeed the creator of everything in the universe, but combined with this is a perpetual insistence on man's moral responsibility and on his need for repentance. Satan is regarded as a fallen angel, and the one who instigates man to sin and sometimes visits him with calamity; but his power is strictly circumscribed, and always subject to divine permission.[9] And while the major emphasis in the Old Testament is on God's sovereignty and holiness, there are many passages which reveal his love.

It is, however, in the proclamation of the apostolic church that the love of God and his divine initiative to save men and women from sin are brought into the sharpest possible focus. Here we are made to see something of the tension in the heart

[9] This is vividly portrayed in the book of Job.

of God himself between his holiness and justice, which must condemn sin, and his compassion and love, which longs to pardon and redeem the sinner – a tension which was only resolved, and could only be resolved, by the unique historical event in which Christ 'died for our sins in accordance with the scriptures'[1]. In this stupendous fact lies the meaning of all the sacrifices prescribed in the Old Testament; and in this the 'righteousness' of God, in 'overlooking' the sins committed in Old Testament times, is manifested or declared.[2] The New Testament, like the Old, believes in Satan, who has a real, although subordinate and circumscribed, power. Nor does the New Testament give us any metaphysical explanation of the origin of evil. It is clear, of course, that God's desire to enjoy fellowship with men and women, and his plan to 'bring many sons to glory',[3] could not have been fulfilled if man was a mere automaton, but only if he was a moral and rational being. This, in its turn, meant that he must be placed in a world of moral choice, in which there was the possibility – indeed, from the point of view of divine fore-knowledge, we should, no doubt, postulate the certainty – that he would make the wrong choice. But the New Testament concentrates on the fact of sin, rather than its origin; and it makes it unmistakably clear that although God allows sin, he never *wills* it. 'God is light, and in him is no (moral) darkness at all';[4] he is not himself tempted by sin, nor does he 'tempt any man',[5] in the sense of solicitation to evil. But he does sometimes put men to the test, and even visit them with judgment; and he does normally allow man's wilfulness and sin to work itself out – even in cruelty, suffering, pain, misery and death which involve not only the sinner himself but many 'innocent' people. This presents us with a mystery to which the Bible gives no adequate explanation; but the unique historical event which gave rise to Christianity at least sheds light in the darkness, for the fact that Christ 'died (and suffered) for our sins' proves that we have no remote Creator who remains aloof, as in Islam, and is not personally involved in human suffering, while the fact that Christ rose

[1] I Cor. 15:3, 4.   [2] Rom. 3:25. *Cf*. Heb. 9:15.
[3] Heb. 2:10.   [4] I Jn. 1:5.   [5] Jas. 1:13.

again on the third day demonstrates the fact that suffering, sin and death will never have the last word.

It is clear, then, that any consideration of the problem of evil necessarily brings us face to face not only with the meaning of human life but with the God – if God there be – who made both man and the world in which he placed him, and who must presumably have a purpose in all he has made and done. But how can we come to any firm and satisfying conclusion about the nature and purposes of God?

To the agnostic this is impossible, and he gives up the struggle in impotence and despair. The deist, on the other hand, virtually goes to the other extreme, and imagines that man can find the solution to all his problems in an intelligent understanding of the natural phenomena of the universe, without any basic need for a divine self-disclosure or for supernatural grace. This is not so very far removed from the attitude of those Hindus who interpret their religion in monistic terms, or those Theravāda Buddhists who believe that men and women struggle on, in the track which Gautama trod, until they too reach the enlightenment which he attained. Such enlightenment might in theory, of course, take the form of an affirmation or a negation – of a belief in a god or gods or an atheistic denial of any supernatural being. But we have already reminded ourselves that St Paul insists that all men in fact know, in their hearts, that there *is* a God – by an inward revelation or disclosure, whether intuitive or rational, based on the phenomenal universe – however much they may succeed in arguing themselves into a convinced and consistent rationalism. Yet this did not, for St Paul, in any way weaken the paramount need for a much fuller and more satisfying divine disclosure, if man was to come to know, in any personal way, the one whose 'everlasting power and deity' he can, without this, only dimly apprehend.

But how could the invisible God so disclose himself to mortal men? To this question the different religions give a wide variety of answers. The very term 'disclose' implies, of course, that the God who so discloses himself cannot be less personal than we are ourselves, although he may well be supra-personal. But this personal God could, in theory at least, reveal himself in a number of different ways. He could do this – and no doubt often has done this – through dreams, visions and voices, whether audible to the ear or only to the heart. In some such terms, presumably, Hindus understand those *avatārs* that mean so much to some of them, in spite of the fact that they may be wholly devoid of any historical foundation. Thus S. Radhakrishnan says that the Upanishads 'belong to *śruti* or revealed literature. They are immemorial, *sanātana*, timeless. Their truths are said to be breathed out by God or visioned by the seers. They are the utterances of the sages who speak out of the fullness of their illumined experience. They are not reached by ordinary perception, inference or reflection, but *seen* by the seers, even as we see and not infer the wealth and riot of colour in the summer sky.'[6] It is in these terms, certainly, that both Jews and Christians believe in the progressive self-disclosure vouchsafed by God through Moses and the prophets. And this same attitude prevails in Islam, where the supreme revelation of the deity is envisaged in terms of direct speech, transmitted to Muḥammad from heaven through the agency of the archangel Gabriel.

Yet again, this divine disclosure may be seen in terms of historical events, in which God intervenes in human history. It was in this way that Jews have always looked back to the Exodus[7] – and to this, too, partial parallels can be found elsewhere. But this involves a very different attitude to the world and to human history than that assumed in many eastern religions. 'Monotheism', as E. L. Allen puts it, 'accepts the world as real, as having a definite origin and moving towards a definite termination at some future date', while for monism 'it is *māyā*, illusory, the present phase in a beginningless and endless series of cycles.[8] Monotheism takes pride in the fact that it has a historical basis . . . it reveres the personality of a founder. For the monisms, general philosophical ideas take the place of historical events . . . A comparison of the two is

---

[6] *The Principal Upanishads*, pp. 22f., quoted in H. D. Lewis and R. L. Slater, *World Religions*, p. 152.

[7] So, of course, have Muslims to the Hijra (Muḥammad's 'flight' from Mecca to Madina, from which Muslims date their era), but in a rather different way.

[8] To the monist, even 'God' is part of *māyā*.

no more possible than a conversation between one who knows only English and another who has only Chinese.'[9] For the criteria by which any alleged self-disclosure of God in history must be judged are first the nature and credibility of the relevant historical event, and then the interpretation that is put upon it.

It is precisely here that the event on which the Christian faith is founded proves to be unique. It can and should be tested as to its historicity by all the scholarly criteria available to us; and it will, in my submission, stand up to the most severely critical examination.[1] As Ferdinand Hahn puts it, in the quest of the historical Jesus 'historical scepticism is altogether inappropriate. In spite of the knowledge that all tradition is already stamped by faith, this tradition still points so clearly back to the history of Jesus that a clear over-all picture arises of the special character of his life and ministry, even when we are not able to produce from it a complete account or a continuous biography.'[2] But the essence of the apostolic *kerygma* concerned not only the life and ministry of Jesus, but also his death and resurrection – as interpreted to them by Old Testament type and prophecy, by their memory of his own predictions of what awaited him and why this must be (grievously though they had failed, at the time, to understand him), by his post-resurrection discourses and explanations and by the illumination given them by the promised Holy Spirit.

In this event it was God himself who took the initiative. It was not man's eternal quest for God, to which all the world's religions bear their testimony. It was not merely a revelation *from* God, such as the Muslim confidently claims. It was, rather, a revelation *of* God,[3] a veritable self-disclosure. It reveals a God who is holy, and therefore hates the sin which inevitably excludes men and women from the fellowship which he longs to have with them; and a God who is love, and was so deeply involved in the world he had created that

[9] E. L. Allen, *Christianity among the Religions*, p. 136.

[1] See my book *Christianity: the Witness of History*.

[2] F. Hahn, in *What can we know about Jesus?*, p. 45.

[3] *Cf.* W. Cantwell Smith, *The Faith of Other Men*, pp. 6of.

he was willing to become man, to share man's life, pain and sorrows, and so to identify himself with man's sin that he actually bore its consequences and penalty on the cross. In retrospect this self-disclosure led, inexorably, to the Christian doctrine of the Trinity. This was no metaphysical abstraction, no product of the imagination of the early church. On the contrary, the apostles and their entourage knew assuredly, from the self-disclosure of God to Israel down the centuries and from the teaching of Jesus himself, that there was only one God; and they continued firmly to believe in the unity of the Godhead. But they were forced by the very facts of their experience to recognize that Jesus was one with God; that the supra-personal God comprehends, in his unity, not only the source and origin of all things, but the eternal Word by which he has always made himself known, and the eternal Spirit by which he energizes and illumines; and that this eternal Word had become incarnate in the Man of Nazareth. And just as the orthodox Muslim, in his dispute with the Mu'tazila about the relation between God and the 'uncreated' Qur'ān, was driven to say that it was neither identical with his essence nor separable from it, so the Fourth Gospel, in a much deeper sense, declares that 'At the beginning God expressed himself. That personal expression, that word, was with God and was God, and he existed with God from the beginning. All creation took place through him, and none took place without him . . . He came into the world – the world he had created – and the world failed to recognize him . . . So the word became a human being and lived among us. We saw his splendour (the splendour as of a father's only son), full of grace and truth . . . It is true that no one has ever seen God at any time. Yet the divine and only Son, who lives in the closest intimacy with the Father, has made him known.'[4]

And the God who so revealed himself is concerned with life as it really is. As Klostermaier puts it: 'the God who appeared in Jesus Christ is where people suffer and struggle and thirst and hunger . . . He is a God indifferent to nothing; on the contrary, he is light and life and the inexorable enemy of

[4] Jn. 1:1-3, 11, 14, 18 (Phillips' translation).

darkness and death. The God manifest in Jesus Christ is not
one who watches from afar but a living God, a God who proves
to the world that there is sin and justice. He is a God become
man not in the circles of pharisees and politicians, but in those
circles where hunger and thirst, toil and work, grief and death,
are well-known. He did not appeal to his divinity but gave his
humanity for his brethren . . . He would not . . . bring the
superficial peace of theological co-existence. He would bring
the sword, the decision, and yet the peace unknown by the
world . . . Men reject him because he unmasks their lies
and hypocrisy, because he cannot be bribed. They would be
willing to place him next to the gods, to offer him incense,
even a little money, to cleanse themselves of sin. They would
like to have him as a statue – but not as a man, not so immediate and provoking.'[5]

In terms of Buddhism we should put the same basic truth a
little differently. Gautama was profoundly moved by human
suffering, and he has always been credited with a deep compassion. But when it comes to how to regard suffering, and
what to do about it, there is all the difference in the world
between 'the serene and passionless Buddha and the tortured
figure on the cross'.[6] He faced the problem just as squarely and
honestly as did Gautama but, instead of seeking to reject, refuse
and eliminate it, he 'took it into himself and felt the fullness
of its bitterness and sorrow; by the grace of God he tasted death
for everyman'. So he suffers with others, and for others; and
he teaches his followers that suffering can be turned into gain.

It is this concept of a suffering Messiah that Muḥammad
utterly repudiated. The Qur'ān is emphatic that the Jews 'say
"We have killed the Messiah, Jesus, son of Mary, the Apostle
of God." But they did not kill him, neither did they crucify
him, but he was counterfeited for them . . . and God took him
up to himself; and God is all-knowing, all-wise.'[7] There has
been much scholarly speculation as to how Muḥammad came
to hold such a view, and a Gnostic source has sometimes been

[5] K. Klostermaier, *Hindu and Christian in Vrindaban*, pp. 49f.
[6] S. C. Neill, *Christian Faith and Other Faiths*, pp. 123f. *Cf.* Charles Eliot,
Hinduism and Buddhism, Vol. I, p. 182.
[7] Sura 4:156. Another translation of the word for 'he was counterfeited'
would be 'it was made to appear so'.

suggested. But Kenneth Cragg is probably[8] right when he
says that the most natural explanation is that Muḥammad
here carried to its logical conclusion the instinctive reaction of
Simon Peter at Caesarea Philippi: namely, that it was no part
of the Messianic office to suffer and die, but rather to triumph
and prevail, and that for God to abandon his chosen messenger to such a death, mere man though he was, would
be a defeat and humiliation for the Almighty. The Muslim,
therefore, feels that he is giving greater honour to Christ, and
greater glory to God, by denying the very possibility of the
crucifixion.

What the Muslim fails to understand at this point is not
only the person of Christ but the nature of God himself.
Far from God abandoning his servant on the cross, it was he
who was there 'in Christ reconciling the world to himself'.
Jesus *was* God manifest in the flesh. And this means that not
only was Jesus just like God, but also the necessary corollary,
that God is just like Jesus. He is a God who comes to men 'not
to be served but to serve', not to take but to give, not to remain aloof but to be involved, not to be indifferent but to
suffer – in a word, to love. To realize this is not to derogate
from the Godhead, but to kneel and worship. Yet the love
of God is never mere sentiment. Just because he loves the
sinner, he hates sin. His love and his judgment are not really
contradictory; on the contrary, his judgment is, in a sense,
the obverse side of his love. But there is, none the less, an inevitable tension between God's love and God's holiness – a
tension which, as we have seen, could only be resolved at the
cross.

[8] All the same, a Basilidian source cannot be discounted, for Irenaeus
tells us that the Basilidians believed that Christ did not himself suffer, but
Simon of Cyrene was crucified in his place. See article on 'Gnosticism' in
A Dictionary of Christian Theology (edited by Alan Richardson, SCM Press,
1969), p. 135. Another possibility is that this is an echo of the Docetic
assertion that only a simulacrum of Jesus was crucified.

5 NO OTHER NAME?

In our second chapter we started from the *kerygma* of the apostolic church and the unique historical event which gave it birth. We saw, first, how this draws a sharp line of distinction between the Christian faith and all those religions which have a mythological origin, or which basically consist in theological or ethical concepts which are essentially independent of the persons, historical or otherwise, to whom they are officially attributed. Equally, it distinguishes Christianity from those religions which look back to some less fundamental historical event – *e.g.* the Exodus from Egypt or the Hijra from Mecca – or which rest on revelations or verbal utterances of God, whatever judgment we may reach as to their authenticity and historicity, which could equally well have been vouchsafed to someone else.

In our third chapter we examined the impact and meaning of this unique historical event from the point of view of Christian experience and compared it with the idea of 'salvation' in other religions and ideologies – whether in terms of this world or of life beyond the grave. We saw that there are, indeed, parallels to some aspects of Christian doctrine in a number of different religions, but that the core and essence of the Christian faith is *sui generis*, for it is directly derived from, and essentially dependent on, the unique event to which it always looks back. And in our last chapter we considered that event once more, this time from the point of view of the light it throws on the nature of God – partly in the context of the baffling, and agonizing, problem of evil, and partly in that of the self-disclosure of God which it essentially provides.

In each of these chapters we described as 'unique' both the

historical event from which we started (and, indeed, from which the Christian faith itself arose) and the salvation and disclosure of the Godhead which flow from it. This was not, of course, intended for a moment to suggest that God has revealed himself in no other way and at no other time. Any such idea would be decisively refuted by the self-disclosure of God in the history of Israel and in the Old Testament scriptures – and it will be our duty, *inter alia*, in this present chapter, to consider what view we should take of the claim that God has in part revealed himself in many different ways and in almost all the world's religions. The term unique is intended to signify that the historical event on which Christianity is founded is itself without parallel, as is also – in its fullness and essential nature – the salvation which it offers and the self-disclosure of God which it enshrines.

This can, I think, be summed up by two quotations. As Edwyn Bevan puts it: 'the great dividing line is that which marks off all those who hold that the relation of Jesus to God – however they describe or formulate it – is of such a kind that it could not be repeated in any other individual – that to speak, in fact, of its being repeated in one *other* individual is a contradiction in terms, since any individual standing in that relation to God would *be* Jesus, and that Jesus, in virtue of this relation, has the same absolute claim upon all men's worship and loyalty as belongs to God. A persuasion of this sort of uniqueness attaching to Jesus seems to me the essential characteristic of what has actually in the field of human history been Christianity.'[1] Similarly, E. O. James asserts that 'the Godhead attributed to the founder of Christianity, alike in the New Testament and by the Church, renders it unique in the history of religion. Nowhere else had it ever been claimed that a historical founder of any religion was the one and only supreme deity'.[2] And the New Testament is emphatic that God's self-disclosure in Jesus was 'once for all'. Teaching may, indeed, be repeated many times, as may also God's verbal messages to man. But his supreme Message, in a life that

[1] E. R. Bevan, *Hellenism and Christianity* (Allen and Unwin, 1921), p. 271 – quoted in E. O. James, *Christianity and Other Religions*, p. 167.
[2] E. O. James, *op. cit.*, p. 170.

was lived and a death that was died, can never be repeated or reproduced.

Inevitably, this is a doctrine which provokes opposition. St Paul himself was under no illusions about this; for he tells us that in his day the 'preaching of the cross' was to the Jews a scandal and to the Greeks an absurdity.[3] Nor is it only the content of the Christian proclamation which men and women, left to themselves, find unacceptable; still more perhaps, in this exceedingly tolerant age, it is its exclusiveness and apparent intolerance which stick in men's throats. In many circles today almost any teaching will be accepted as at least a possible contribution to the truth provided only that it does not include any denial of the validity of other contributions – however mutually incompatible these different contributions may be. As Francis Schaeffer insists, the logic of thesis and antithesis has been abandoned in favour of a comprehensive, but wholly illogical, synthesis.[4]

But in this matter synthesis is not a viable option. It is, of course, a common experience for a Christian to learn much from men of other faiths – in devotion, humility, courage and a host of other virtues; and it is perfectly possible for him to learn from the teaching of some other religion a lesson he has failed to learn from his own. But this is a very different matter from the sort of synthesis which aspires to construct a syncretic religion. We have already discussed this subject in the introductory chapter of this book. In short, the Christian answer, as I see it, must always be: 'Dialogue, yes; syncretism, no.' For if God could have *adequately* revealed himself in any other way, how can one possibly believe he would have gone to the almost unbelievable lengths of the incarnation? This was no mere theophany, we must remind ourselves; no mere appearance of God among men, as a Hindu believes to have happened in an *avatār*. It was God actually *becoming* man, with all that this must necessarily have involved. And if God could have dealt with the problem of evil in any other way whatever, how can one possibly believe that he would, in Christ, himself have taken the sinner's place and borne the sinner's

[3] See 1 Cor. 1:23.
[4] *Cf.* F. A. Schaeffer, *Escape from Reason* (Inter-Varsity Press, 1968), p. 41.

guilt – with all the agony (to say nothing of the mystery), expressed in that cry of dereliction from the cross: 'My God, my God, why hast thou forsaken me?'[5]

Inevitably, then, the Christian faith is either itself false or 'casts the shadow of falsehood, or at least of imperfect truth, on every other system. This Christian claim' – as Stephen Neill insists – 'is naturally offensive to the adherents of every other religious system. It is almost as offensive to modern man, brought up in the atmosphere of relativism, in which tolerance[6] is regarded almost as the highest of the virtues. But we must not suppose that this claim to universal validity is something that can quietly be removed from the Gospel without changing it into something entirely different from what it is. The mission of Jesus was limited to the Jews and did not look immediately beyond them; but his life, his method and his message do not make sense, unless they are interpreted in the light of his own conviction that he was in fact the final and decisive word of God to men . . . For the human sickness there is one specific remedy, and this is it. There is no other.'[7]

This seems to me to be the clear import of the teaching of the Bible. There are a number of relevant verses which demand consideration in this context. But some, I think, are more fundamental than others.

One verse which used to be cited in this connection is John 10:8, where Jesus is quoted as having said: 'All who came before me are thieves and robbers; but the sheep did not heed them.' At first sight this would certainly appear to be a singularly sweeping and categorical statement, which might be thought to include in its condemnation all previous religious teachers without exception. But it clearly cannot, in fact, have any such far-ranging import, for it is unthinkable that Jesus should have included Moses, Abraham, David or John the Baptist, for example – to all of whom he bore witness else-

---

[5] Mk. 15:34.
[6] Tolerance as a social policy is a lesson we have, happily, at least begun to learn. To attempt to *force* on others what we believe to be true is manifestly wrong. But this sort of tolerance should not be confused with 'relativism', or the intellectual flabbiness which sees no essential distinction between truth and error.
[7] S. C. Neill, *Christian Faith and Other Faiths*, pp. 16, 17.

where as having actually testified of him – in such a denunciation. The words must be governed by the definition of 'a thief
and a robber' given just before; namely, 'he who does not enter
the sheepfold by the door but climbs in by another way'[8] –
and this *could* in theory, I suppose, refer to all those who had
made false Messianic claims or bogus pretensions to being
'saviours'. But this particular discourse can best be understood in the light of the controversy with some of the Pharisees
which immediately precedes it. It is almost certain that Jesus
must have had the false shepherds of Ezekiel 34 in mind; and
there the denunciation is clearly addressed to unfaithful
Jewish rulers. As R. H. Lightfoot puts it: 'It is a basic tenet of
this gospel that the true leaders of Israel, from Abraham and
Moses to John the Baptist, looked forward to the coming of
the Lord and bore witness to Him; hence there is obviously no
reference in this verse to them, or indeed to any forerunner of
the Lord who could be said to have partaken, in any way, of
the divine Logos . . . Rather, the verse is a very strong expression, in negative form, of the fact that all truth is now
present in the incarnate Lord.'[9]

It is unlikely, then, that the founders and teachers of other
religions were in fact within the meaning and intention of
these words. The phrase 'thieves and robbers' clearly implies an
intention to take – whether by stealth or force – what belongs
to another, so it would scarcely be applicable to one who, in all
sincerity, gave teaching which he thought (however mis-
takenly) to be true; but it *could* certainly apply to one who
claimed to be a saviour when in fact he knew he was not.
Yet it is significant that W. Hendriksen considers it unrealistic
to think here even of false Messiahs who had arisen before
the beginning of Christ's ministry. The context, he asserts,
'says nothing about them. Without any question, it would
seem to us, Jesus is thinking here of the men who are standing
right in front of him as he is speaking, namely, the religious
leaders of the people, the members of the Sanhedrin, Sadducees and Pharisees, but especially the latter (see 9:40; 10:19).
They were the ones who were trying, by means of intimidation

[8] Jn. 10:1.   [9] R. H. Lightfoot, *St. John's Gospel. A Commentary*. Edited by
C. F. Evans (Oxford University Press, 1956), p. 210.

(9:22), to steal the people, and thus to gain honour for themselves in an illegitimate manner. If threats were insufficient,
they would use violence. They were, indeed, both thieves and
robbers. Moreover, they were already on the scene when
Jesus came into the world . . . Hence, it is easy to understand
why Jesus says that they had come *before* him. It is also understandable that Jesus says, "*are* (not *were*) thieves and robbers."
They had not disappeared, but were still present.'[1] It is also
noteworthy that this verse ends with the explicit assertion that
'the sheep did not heed' these thieves and robbers, which
again may well be taken to limit the import of the denunciation
to false teachers among the Jews. But it is only fair to add that
Westcott, while he too believes that the use of the present
tense about the thieves and robbers 'fixes the application of the
words to the immediate crisis of national expectation' (and to
those 'who made themselves "doors" of approach to God
(Mat. 23:14) . . . and continued to be inspired by selfishness'),
goes on to say that 'we may also see a wider application of the
phrase to all non-Jewish religions or philosophical systems
which claimed to bring final and perfect satisfaction to men
. . . The condemnation does not touch "seekers after God."
These were seekers after self.'[2]

Considerably more central to our subject are the words in
John 14:6: 'I am the way, and the truth, and the life; no one
comes to the Father, but by me.' Here the import of the first
half of the verse is clear enough: it constitutes an unequivocal
affirmation that in the incarnate Lord, uniquely, men can find
the road to God, the truth about God, and the life of God.
It is the utterly exclusive claim of the second part of the verse
which gives us pause: that there is no other way whatever.
And with this we may couple the categorical statement in the
Synoptic tradition that 'no one knows the Father except
the Son and any one to whom the Son chooses to reveal
him',[3] and also the stern warning in 1 John 2:23: 'No one who

---

[1] W. Hendriksen, *The Gospel of John* (Banner of Truth Trust. Second
British Edition, 1961), pp. 108f.
[2] B. F. Westcott, *The Gospel according to St. John* (John Murray, 1908),
Vol. II, pp. 53f.
[3] Mt. 11:27. *Cf.* Lk. 10:22. This is, in fact, part of the tradition commonly
attributed to 'Q'.

denies the Son has the Father. He who confesses the Son has the Father also.' It may be that John A. T. Robinson is right when he suggests that the primary purpose of John's Gospel was to lead the Jews of the Dispersion to faith in Jesus as the Christ, the Son of God, while that of the Epistles of John was to warn Jews of the Dispersion who had already come to faith in Christ against the tragedy of falling into apostasy.[4] But while this might explain the emphasis on the element of denial in the last of these verses, it can scarcely alter the import of the exclusive claim which is common to them all.

Taken by themselves, the thrust of these verses might conceivably be softened by the argument that what they basically assert is that no-one can come to know God *as Father* except through Christ the Son, rather than that no-one can come to know God at all except through him. In point of fact, however, they do not stand alone, but must be read in conjunction with the apostolic proclamation in Acts 4:12 that 'there is salvation in no one else, for there is no other name under heaven given among men by which we must be saved'. It is, of course, perfectly in order to observe that in the Bible the 'name' of God or Christ is often used as a synonym for his revealed character; but I cannot see that this makes any significant difference in this context. It seems to me that the consistent teaching of these verses as a whole – indeed, their necessary and inescapable import – is that it is *only* through Christ that any man can come to a personal knowledge of, and fellowship with, God, and *only* through his life, death and resurrection that any man can come to an experience of salvation. To quote Stephen Neill once more: 'For the human sickness there is one specific remedy, and this is it. There is no other.'

But the question immediately arises as to how, precisely, this applies to those who came before Christ – to Abraham, Moses, David and John the Baptist, for example. And if it is answered that each of these came to know God, and to enjoy his forgiveness and fellowship, through the Christ whose coming they in part discerned and to whom they all bore

[4] *Cf.* J. A. T. Robinson, *Twelve New Testament Studies* (SCM Press, 1962), pp. 107–138.

testimony, then what of the multitude of repentant and believing Jews who can scarcely be thought to have had any such
vivid spiritual perception of what God was going to do in the
future? Here, as it seems to me, there can be only one answer:
that when an Israelite came to realize that he was a sinner,
when he turned to God in repentance and faith, and when he
brought his sin offering,[5] he was in fact accepted and forgiven
– *not* on the basis of the animal sacrifice he had brought, but on
the basis of what that sacrifice foreshadowed. The Old Testament sacrifices pointed forward to what God himself did in
Christ, the Lamb of God, when he died on the cross for sinful
men. That David, for example, did enjoy this forgiveness as a
conscious experience St Paul clearly teaches[6] and is unmistakably apparent in the Psalms he wrote; and animal sacrifices could never take away human sins. Indeed, an essential
element in the propitiation Christ made on the cross was,
the apostle tells us, that 'God meant by this to demonstrate
his justice, because in his forbearance he had overlooked the
sins of the past'[7] – for the moral basis on which forgiveness
was always available was the redemption finally effected in
Christ.

It seems clear, then, that believing Jews under the Old
Testament dispensation enjoyed forgiveness and salvation
through that saving work of God in Christ (dated, of course,
according to the calendars of men, but timeless and eternal
in its divine significance) by which alone a holy God can and
does forgive the repentant sinner – little though most of them
can have understood this. But is there no other sense than this
in which we can say that it was through Christ that they came
to know God? Surely, here, we must think of the pre-incar-
nate Son as the Word who was in the beginning with God
and was God, through whom alone all things that exist came
into being,[8] who was the life that was the light of men[9] and
the true light which illumines every man.[1] It is significant, too,
that St Paul speaks of the Israelites as having drunk 'from the

[5] Or, in the case of those major moral sins for which no provision was made
in the sacrificial system, when he pleaded for forgiveness as David did in
Psalm 51.
[6] Rom. 4:7, 8.   [7] Rom. 3:25, NEB. Heb. 9:15 is even more explicit.
[8] Jn. 1:1,2.   [9] Jn. 1:14.   [1] Jn. 1:9.

supernatural Rock which followed them, and the Rock was Christ',[2] while St Peter declares that it was the 'spirit of Christ' who, through the prophets, was predicting his coming passion.[3] In the case of Abraham, Jesus himself said that he 'saw my day and was glad'.[4] In view, moreover, of the positive and categorical assertion in the Fourth Gospel that 'No one has ever seen God; but God's only son, he who is nearest to the Father's heart, he has made him known',[5] we must conclude that the One who spoke with Moses 'face to face', and who granted him a partial vision of his form, must have been the Second Person of the Trinity. This is also true, presumably, of the 'Angel' – or the 'Angel of the Lord' – who is virtually identified with God himself in a number of Old Testament passages.

What, then, was the difference between the experience of believers in Old Testament times and that of Christians under the New Covenant? It was not that godly Jews were saved by 'works' or by their obedience to the law, for no-one can ever be saved by 'works' and no Jew ever succeeded in keeping the law. Believers under the Old Covenant were saved by grace through faith, just as we are: that is, through the grace of God in Christ. But they (if I may here deliberately, but perhaps excusably, misquote Scripture) saw 'in a mirror dimly' (or, as the NEB puts it, 'puzzling reflections in a mirror'), while we, comparatively speaking, already see 'face to face'.[6] Under the Old Covenant they had 'but a shadow, and no true image, of the good things which were to come', and had to offer 'the same sacrifices year after year' which could never 'bring the worshippers to perfection',[7] while we know 'the offering of the body of Jesus Christ once and for all',[8] and a forgiveness which excludes any further offering for sin and brings assurance of both heart and conscience. Their knowledge was deficient, their assurance often fitful, but their forgiven status identical with ours. But how ashamed we should be when we compare the poverty of our own actual experience of God with that of Enoch, Abraham, David or Daniel.

[2] 1 Cor. 10:4.   [3] 1 Pet. 1:11.   [4] Jn. 8:56.
[5] Jn. 1:18, NEB.   [6] 1 Cor. 13:12.
[7] Heb. 10:1, NEB.   [8] Heb. 10:10, NEB.

So far, then, the teaching of the Bible seems clear enough. But there remain a number of difficult problems with which we must attempt to grapple. And the first and most perplexing, which must inevitably occur to each one of us at this point, is simply this: if the only way to God is through Christ, and the only basis of forgiveness and acceptance the atonement effected at the cross, then what about all those countless millions of people in the world today – to say nothing of the millions who have already lived and died – who, through no fault of their own, have never heard of the only mediator and only Saviour? Are they utterly without hope, as many of our missionary forebears firmly believed? That would be an agonizing thought. Yet it would be a denial of the biblical teaching we have just considered to reply, as many do, that they will be judged and justified by a different standard, according to the 'light' or truth which was in fact available to them. This is true, no doubt, in so far as the standard by which they will be judged is concerned; for we have St Paul's authority for the premise that, whereas the Jew will be judged on the basis of the Law revealed on Sinai, non-Jews will be judged according to the criterion of the requirements of the law 'inscribed on their hearts'.[9] The most elementary principles of justice would, indeed, seem to demand this; but I cannot see that it provides any sort of solution to our problem. For the fact remains that, just as no Jew has ever succeeded in keeping the Mosaic Law or the injunctions of the prophets, so no non-Jew has ever succeeded in living up to the standard of the moral and ethical principles according to which he knows that he ought to regulate his conduct. We only need to turn from the second to the third chapter of the Epistle to the Romans to read that 'no human being can be justified in the sight of God' on the basis of law, whatever that law may be, for 'law brings only the consciousness of sin'.[1] To this there can be no exception. The verdict of God is explicit and unequivocal – that 'all have sinned and fall short of the glory of God'.[2]

So our problem comes down to this: is there any basis on

which the efficacy of the one atonement can avail those who have never heard about it? It is not enough to say, along with Wilfred Cantwell Smith, that 'a Buddhist who is saved, or a Hindu or a Muslim or whoever, is saved, and is saved only, because God is the kind of God whom Jesus Christ has revealed Him to be'.[3] This is clearly true, so far as it goes – for the character and nature of the God with whom we have to do is fundamental. But his character, as revealed in the Bible (and, indeed, in Christ himself), does not solely and only consist in a profound and universal benevolence. God is 'light' as well as 'love', 'justice' as well as 'mercy', and to concentrate on the one quality alone is not only to distort his character but to caricature the essence of divine love itself. God's hatred of sin is, in reality, the inevitable concomitant of his love for the sinner: the reverse side of the very same coin. It is gloriously true that God 'desires all men to be saved and to come to the knowledge of the truth',[4] but this can only be through the Saviour who is himself 'the propitiation for our sins: and not for ours only, but also for the sins of the whole world'.[5]

So again we come back to the same question: how can this come about if they have never heard of the only Saviour? It is precisely here, as I see it, that we may find a ray of light by going back to what we have already said about those multitudes of Jews who, in Old Testament times, turned to God in repentance, brought the prescribed sacrifice,[6] and threw themselves on his mercy. It was not that they *earned* that mercy by their repentance or obedience, or that an animal sacrifice could ever avail to atone for human sin. It was that their repentance and faith (themselves, of course, the result of God's work in their hearts) opened the gate, as it were, to the grace, mercy and forgiveness which he always longed to extend to them, and which was to be made for ever available at the cross on which Christ 'gave himself a ransom for all, to be testified in due time'.[7] May we not believe, then, that the

[3] W. Cantwell Smith, *The Faith of Other Men*, p. 126.

[4] 1 Tim. 2:4, RSV.

[5] 1 Jn. 2:2, AV.

[6] Where, indeed, any sacrifice was appropriate. For major moral sins, as we have seen, no sacrifice was prescribed.

[7] 1 Tim. 2:6, AV.

same would be true of the follower of some other religion in whose heart the God of all mercy had been working by his Spirit, who had come in some measure to realize his sin and need for forgiveness, and who had been enabled, in the twilight as it were, to throw himself on the mercy of God? Is not this, perhaps, the meaning of St Peter's words in the house of Cornelius: 'I now see how true it is that God has no favourites, but that in every nation the man who is godfearing and does what is right is acceptable to him.'[8] This cannot mean that the man who tries to be religious and strives to be moral will earn salvation, for the whole Bible denies this possibility. But does it not mean that the man who realizes something of his sin or need, and throws himself on the mercy of God with a sincerity which shows itself in his life (which would always, of course, be a sure sign of the inward prompting of God's Spirit, and especially so in the case of one who had never heard the gospel), would find that mercy – although without understanding it – at the cross on which Christ 'died for all'?[9]

'The Apostle', writes G. Campbell Morgan commenting on this passage, 'did not mean to say that man is received upon the basis of his morality', for he can be saved only by what God did, in Christ, at the cross. 'But no man is to be saved because he understands the doctrine of the Atonement. He is saved, not by understanding it, but because he fears God and works righteousness' – and he goes on to describe 'the glad and glorious surprise' with which, at the last day, we shall find that there are those who have 'walked in the light they had, and wrought righteousness, and were acceptable to Him; not because of their morality, but by the infinite merit of the Cross'.[1] But it is essential, I think, that we should here interpret the phrase 'walked in the light they had' in terms of that sense of need, and that casting of themselves on the mercy of God, to which I have already referred. This, too, must have been what Zwingli meant when he wrote (in somewhat sweeping terms): 'In short, there has not lived a single good

---

[8] Acts 10:34, 35, NEB.
[9] 2 Cor. 5:14, RSV.
[1] G. Campbell Morgan, *The Acts of the Apostles* (Pickering & Inglis, 1945), p. 220.

man, there has not been a single pious heart or believing soul from the beginning of the world to the end, which you will not see there in the presence of God.'[2]

Can we doubt, moreover, that God is able to speak directly to the human heart, and particularly so when neither human messenger nor printed page is available to bear their testimony? What of Melchizedek or Balaam, for example, in the Old Testament, who from outside the covenant people clearly heard and obeyed (or, in Balaam's case, in part obeyed) the voice of God? What of the warnings given in dreams to such persons as Nebuchadnezzar and Abimelech? What, indeed, of the call of Abraham the Aramaean?

This, in any case, has been my own belief for some years, and I have recently been interested and encouraged to find that not only Zwingli and Campbell Morgan, but also George Goodman,[3] held substantially the same view. It has been expounded by the latter fully – and, to me at least, in a way which is *in general* convincing – in a booklet entitled *The Heathen. Their Present State and Future Destiny*[4] which is now unhappily out of print. He argues that it is contrary to both Scripture and experience to suggest that those of other religions have no knowledge whatever of either sin or of God, and quotes in support the confession of Seneca ('We are all wicked; what we blame in another each will find in his own bosom') and of Horace ('I see and approve the better course – I follow the worse'). He also points to the sense of sin and need which must sometimes, surely, provide the motive force for the pilgrimages men make, the fasts they endure, the lacerations they inflict on themselves, and the penances they perform, whether on their own behalf or that of others. St Paul himself tells us that all men know something of the judgment of God on sin and that most treat this judgment with scorn;[5] but it seems clear that there are some who cry out to him for forgive-

[2] *Zwingli and Bullinger* (Library of Christian Classics, SCM Press, 1953), p. 276.
[3] Another Bible teacher who was a well-known speaker, in his day, at the Keswick Convention, and belonged to what are now called the 'Christian Brethren'.
[4] Pickering and Inglis.
[5] Rom. 1:32.

ness and even retain – perhaps from a primitive revelation –
the conviction that the expiation of sin must be by means of a
sacrifice of some kind. Often, indeed, men are prepared to
undergo much self-denial to provide the sacrifices they believe
to be acceptable. This is *not*, of course, to argue that this in
itself is enough to save them; for there is only one way of
salvation, and of this they have never heard; nor have they
(or anyone else) always walked even in the light they had.
Like us they are sinners. 'Together we stand before God alike
in this (we with the fuller light and they in comparative
darkness), guilty, sin-bound, and lost, unable to save or justify
ourselves.' Our only hope is grace, and that on the basis of
what God himself did in Christ at the cross. And this is their
only hope, too.

But is this grace ever extended, he asks, apart from any
knowledge of the truth as this is revealed in the gospel? Does
ignorance disqualify for grace? 'If so, where in Scripture do
we have the exact amount of knowledge required set out?'
For *assurance*, no doubt, knowledge is required, but 'for grace
it is not so much knowledge as a right attitude towards God
that matters'. So if, by reason of the inner working of God's
Spirit, a man or woman really cries out for the mercy of
God, will they not find it? 'Shall not grace flow out to them
and the gift of grace, even though knowledge and assurance
and the personal enjoyment of deliverance await the arrival
of the evangelist?' So he suggests that it is *possible* that an
omniscient God will judge those who have never heard of
Christ on the basis of what he knows would have been their
response if they had heard[6] – manifested, in their ignorance,
by that self-despair and abandonment to God's mercy to
which his Spirit alone can have brought them, for true
self-despair and abandonment to God's mercy can be explained in no other way.

There are, moreover, many unequivocal statements in both
the Old and New Testaments about those who 'seek' God. In
the book of Lamentations we read that the Lord is good to
all who seek him,[7] and the writer of Proverbs insists that
'those who seek me diligently find me'.[8] It is true that the

[6] *Cf.* Lk. 10:13.   [7] La. 3:25, NEB.   [8] Pr. 8:17, RSV.

Psalmist tells us that when God 'looks down from heaven on all mankind to see if any act wisely, if any seek out God', he finds that 'all are unfaithful, all are rotten to the core'[9] – and St Paul adds that there is 'no one who seeks God'.[1] But in the light of our Lord's positive statement that 'everyone who asks receives, he who seeks finds, and to him who knocks, the door will be opened'[2] this must, presumably, be interpreted as meaning that no man seeks with his whole heart, or in any way which would *merit* salvation, and that no-one seeks at all apart from divine grace. God made man, St Paul told the Athenians, that he should seek him 'and, it might be, touch and find him'[3] and added 'though indeed he is not far from each one of us, for in him we live and move, in him we exist'; while the writer of the Epistle to the Hebrews emphasizes that one of the basic marks of faith is to believe that God 'rewards those who seek him'.[4] So the essential elements would seem to be a God-given sense of sin or need, and a self-abandonment to God's mercy.

If a man of whom this is true subsequently hears and understands the gospel, then I myself believe that he would be among the company of those, whom one does sometimes meet on the mission field, who welcome and accept it at once, saying (in effect): 'This is what I have been waiting for all these years. Why didn't you come and tell me before?' And if he never hears the gospel here on earth, then I suppose that he will wake up, as it were, on the other side of the grave to worship the One in whom, without understanding it at the time, he had found the mercy of God.

I have recently discussed this point with a well-known writer on comparative religion who emphasizes, just as I do, that salvation can be only through Christ; who has struggled with this same problem of whether – and if so how – that salvation is available to those who, through no fault of their own, have never heard of him; but who takes a more subjective view of the atonement than I do – and he insists that there must be an after-death experience of the transforming power

[9] Ps. 53:2, 3, NEB. *Cf.* Ps. 14:2, 3.   [1] Rom. 3:11, NEB.
[2] Lk. 11:9, 10, NEB. *Cf.* Mt. 7:7, 8.   [3] Acts 17:27, NEB.
[4] Heb. 11:6, RSV.

of Christ's love. He asserts, reasonably enough, that this cannot properly be termed a 'Second Chance', for it represents – at least from one point of view – a first and only chance. But for such a 'chance', whatever one may call it, I can find no warrant whatever in Scripture. Nor do I myself see the need for it; for I believe that if in this world a man has really, as a result of the prompting and enabling of the Holy Spirit, thrown himself on the mercy of God (like the 'publican' in the Temple who cried out 'God be merciful to me, a sinner'), that mercy will already have reached him on the basis of the propitiation which has been made 'once for all' – and (like the publican again) he will have been 'justified'.[5] With much less knowledge he has taken up the same position as the publican who 'did not deserve forgiveness on account of his submissive prayer, but through his self-despising confession of guilt was in a condition to receive the forgiveness granted by God to the penitent. For . . . the publican the general rule held good that . . . he who really humbles himself (with sincere confession of guilt) will be exalted.'[6] What will happen to him beyond the grave can best be described, as I see it, as an adoring recognition of his Saviour and comprehension of what he owes to him.

Nor should this view, if it be correct, lead to any diminution of missionary urgency. First, we are under orders, explicit and unequivocal, to go to all the world with the good news. Secondly, a man such as we have discussed may indeed have found God's mercy, but desperately needs teaching, heart assurance, and a message he can communicate to others. Perhaps this is the meaning of the verse in the Benedictus which speaks of giving '*knowledge* of salvation to his people in the forgiveness of their sins'.[7] Possibly, again, this is in part the meaning of the Lord's special message to St Paul in Corinth: 'Do not be afraid, but speak . . . for I have many people in this city.'[8] On this Campbell Morgan comments that God 'knew the heartache and the agony of many in

[5] It is, perhaps, significant that even the publican does not seem to have reached real assurance. See Lk. 18:9–14.
[6] *Cf.* N. Geldenhuys, *Commentary on the Gospel of Luke* (Marshall, Morgan & Scott, 1950), p. 451.
[7] Lk. 1:77.   [8] Acts 18:9, 10.

NO OTHER NAME? 107

Corinth – the longing of many, inarticulate, not understood,
for exactly that which he (the apostle) had to minister and to
give'. The words were not spoken of those who were already
Christians, but of 'those whom his Lord numbered among His
own'.[9] Thirdly, if we consider what enabled us ourselves to
give up attempting to earn salvation and throw ourselves on
the mercy of God, would we not – almost invariably – say
that it was hearing the good news of what Christ had done,
the very message which the apostle was commanded to preach
in Corinth? So it is enormously important that we, too, should
go and tell others this same message. Fourthly, can we deny
others the present experience of joy, peace and power which
a conscious knowledge of Christ, and communion with him,
alone can bring? As for our own spiritual responsibility
vis-à-vis the gospel, this is crystal clear, for we have heard of
the only Saviour, so 'how shall we escape if we neglect such a
great salvation?'[1]

But a further problem also confronts us: what view must
the Christian take of other religions as systems? Broadly
speaking, three main views have been – and still are – held
by Christians on this subject. First, there are those who,
impressed by the elements of truth that can be found in most,
if not all, other religions, and by the devotion and virtue of
some of their adherents, regard them as a sort of *praeparatio
evangelica* – as, indeed, all Christians would say of Old Testament Judaism. Christ, therefore, comes 'not to destroy but to
fulfil'; and the convert ought to feel that 'he has lost nothing
but has gained much, and that in particular all that was true
in his old allegiance has been preserved' – and, indeed, en-
hanced – 'in the new'.[2]

Some who take this view would, as we have seen, explain
the elements of truth in other religions in terms of an original
revelation which has never been wholly lost or forgotten.
Others, again, would discern in them the work of Christ
himself, as the eternal Logos and the 'light that enlightens
every man'. It is he, they would say, who 'bears witness to,
makes manifest, the eternal truth which is written on the

[9] G. Campbell Morgan, *The Acts of the Apostles*, pp. 334f.
[1] Heb. 2:3, RSV.   [2] E. L. Allen, *Christianity among the Religions*, p. 123.

heart of man as such'.[3] As William Temple put it: 'By the word of God – that is to say by Jesus Christ – Isaiah and Plato, Zoroaster, Buddha, and Confucius uttered and wrote such truths as they declared. There is only one Divine Light, and every man in his own measure is enlightened by it.'[4] This view was held by Justin Martyr and the Christian philosophers of Alexandria in the second and third centuries,[5] and has been adopted by many others down the years. In E. L. Allen's summary of Schelling's thought, Christ 'was present in every age to every race, but he was not known as such. Heathenism is related to Christianity as law to gospel, reason to faith, nature to grace. The heathen is like a blind man, feeling the sun's warmth but not seeing the sun itself. Christ was within heathenism as natural potency but not yet as personal principle.'[6] It was only when the Word was made flesh, however, that he could be known as a personal Saviour and Lord.

The second view which has been taken by Christians about other religions is the diametrical opposite of this: namely that they do not emanate in any sense from God, but from the devil. Prominence is given, therefore, to the darker side of their ethical teaching and the more debased elements in their theological concepts; and those rays of truth which they indubitably contain are explained in terms of the fact that even Satan himself can and does sometimes appear as an angel of light. A primary emphasis is put on the basic fact that they inevitably deny – whether by explicit statement, as in Islam, or by implicit teaching, as in the great pre-Christian religions the unique claims of the 'Word made flesh', and that they hold themselves out, as it were, as substitutes for and alternatives to the only gospel that can save and satisfy.

The third view sees these religions as not so much divine revelation, nor yet Satanic deception, but as human aspiration – as man's attempts (whether more or less enlightened) to solve the mysteries of life. Among those who take this view

[3] *Ibid.*, p. 35, summarizing the view of Sebastian Frank.
[4] W. Temple, *Readings in St John's Gospel*, Vol. 1, p. 10.
[5] *Cf.* E. C. Dewick, *The Christian Attitude to Other Religions*, p. 120.
[6] E. L. Allen, *op. cit.*, p. 70.

there are two possible attitudes with regard to Christianity. Some would regard it as no more than the nearest approximation to ultimate truth, man's highest attainment in the age-long evolution of religion. Others would go much further than this, and believe it to be the one and only divine self-disclosure (with Judaism, of course, as a forerunner), in which God himself came down from heaven, as it were, to reveal himself to man, while all the other religions represent human attempts to climb up to heaven to discover God.

I cannot, myself, opt for any one of these three views *simpliciter*, for there is, I believe, some truth in each. The non-Christian religions seem to me to resemble a patchwork quilt, with brighter and darker components in differing proportions. There are elements of truth which must come from God himself, whether through the memory of an original revelation or through that measure of self-disclosure which, I cannot doubt, God still vouchsafes to those who truly seek him.[7] But there are also elements which are definitely false, and which I, for one, cannot doubt come from the 'father of lies' – whose primary purpose is not so much to entice men into sensual sin as to keep them back, by any means in his power, from the only Saviour. Yet again, there is much that could best be described as human aspirations after the truth, rather than either divine revelation or Satanic deception.

But is there, as some would assert, any 'saving structure' in these other religions? Can we say, with W. Cantwell Smith, that after studying some of these religions, and after fellowship with some of their adherents, we have to recognize that these religious traditions are 'channels through which God Himself comes into touch with these His children'?[8] Can we say, with Raymond Panikkar, that the 'good and bona fide Hindu is saved by Christ and not by Hinduism, but it is through the sacraments of Hinduism, through the message of morality and the good life, through the mysterion that comes down to him through Hinduism, that Christ saves the Hindu normally'?[9] For myself, I could not go nearly so far as this, and

[7] *Cf.* pp. 101ff. above. [8] W. Cantwell Smith, *The Faith of Other Men*, p. 124. [9] R. Panikkar, *The Unknown Christ of Hinduism* (Darton, Longman and Todd, 1965), p. 54.

think there is much more truth in another dictum of Cantwell Smith: 'If there is any truth in the Buddhist tradition, then its truth is not "in Buddhism", it is in the nature of things'[1] – for we are all one in our basic human need. I have heard of more than one Muslim whose study of the Qur'ān made him seek after Christ;[2] but I think we must ascribe this to the Spirit of God, or, as John puts it, the 'light that enlightens every man',[3] meeting him in his need, rather than attribute it to the Qur'ān as such. Yet there are certainly elements in non-Christian religions – and, indeed, in the heart of man – which testify in some measure, as George Goodman suggests, to the righteousness and judgment of God, to the sin and guilt of man, and to the need of men and women everywhere for expiation and forgiveness.

In other words, God has never left himself wholly without witness in his self-disclosures to mankind.[4] This is true even of those who stifle or 'suppress' the truth, as St Paul insists.[5] It is true of the Muslim, who believes passionately in one true God, however much we may regard his concept of that God as in some sense a caricature of the 'God and Father of our Lord Jesus Christ' – for I have never met a Muslim convert who regards the God he previously sought to worship as a wholly false God; instead, he is filled with wonder and gratitude that he has now been brought to know that God as he really is, in Jesus Christ our Lord. And this is still more evident in converted Jews who, like St Paul before Felix, testify (in one phrase or another) that according to the 'Way', which other Jews called a sect, they now worship the God of their fathers,[6] uniquely and finally revealed in their promised Messiah. 'This element of continuity', Lesslie Newbigin writes, 'is confirmed in the experience of many who have become converts to Christianity from other religions. Even though this conversion involves a radical discontinuity, yet there is often the strong conviction afterwards that it was the

[1] W. Cantwell Smith, *op. cit.*, p. 81.
[2] *E.g.* a certain Mallam Ibrāhīm, who was crucified in the market place in Kano some 80 years ago.
[3] Jn. 1:9.
[4] *Cf.* E. O. James, *Christianity and Other Religions*, p. 154. Also Acts 14:17.
[5] Rom. 1:18.   [6] Acts 24:14.

living and true God who was dealing with them in the days of their pre-Christian wrestlings.'[7]

But now, in Christ, the one eternal God has actually become man. He has not merely visited humanity, he has taken our very nature. Now there is only one teacher, one Lord, one shepherd, one mediator.[8] He has a name which is above every name. 'In no one else can salvation be found. For in all the world no other name has been given to men but this, and it is by this name that we must be saved!'[9] So the attitude of the Christian to men of other religions can only be the attitude of the 'witness who points to the one Lord Jesus Christ as the Lord of all men . . . The Church does not apologise for the fact that it wants all men to know Jesus Christ and to follow him. Its very calling is to proclaim the Gospel to the ends of the earth. It cannot make any restrictions in this respect. Whether people have a high, a low or a primitive religion, whether they have sublime ideals or a defective morality makes no fundamental difference in this respect. All must hear the Gospel.'[1]

And this is a call for radical repentance and conversion. 'When the people heard the first Christian preaching they were cut to the heart and said to Peter: "What shall we do?" Peter said, "Repent, be baptized every one of you in the name of Jesus Christ for the forgiveness of your sins and you shall receive the Holy Spirit. The promise is to you and your children and to all that are afar off, every one whom the Lord calls." That does not mean, however, that the promise does not need to be accepted. There is an RSVP on this card. "And those who received the word were baptized . . . and they devoted themselves to the apostles' teaching and fellowship, to the breaking of the bread and the prayers." '[2]

[7] L. Newbigin, *The Finality of Christ*, p. 59.
[8] *Cf.* W. A. Visser 't Hooft, *No Other Name*, p. 96.
[9] Acts 4:12, Phillips.
[1] W. A. Visser 't Hooft, *op. cit.*, p. 116.
[2] L. Newbigin, *op. cit.*, p. 99.

BIBLIOGRAPHY

(*This is not a reading list, but is confined to books to which reference has in fact been made in the text or footnotes.*)

Allegro, John, *The Sacred Mushroom and the Cross* (Hodder and Stoughton), 1970.

Allen, E. L., *Christianity among the Religions* (Allen and Unwin), 1960.

Anderson, J. N. D., *Christianity: the Witness of History* (Tyndale Press), 1969.

Anderson, J. N. D. (editor), *The World's Religions*. 2nd ed. (Inter-Varsity Fellowship), 1951.

Aurobindo, Sri, *Essays on the Gītā* (Aurobindo Library, Madras and New York), 1950.

Basham, A. L., *The Wonder that was India* (Sidgwick and Jackson), 1954.

Bevan, E. R., *Hellenism and Christianity* (Allen and Unwin), 1921.

Bevan, E. R., *The History of Christianity in the Light of Modern Knowledge* (Butterworth), 1929.

Bornkamm, Günther (with Ferdinand Hahn and Wenzel Lohff), *What can we know about Jesus?* Translated by G. Foley (St Andrew Press), 1969.

Brandon, S. G. F., *Man and his Destiny in the Great Religions* (Manchester University Press), 1962.

Bromiley, G. W. (editor), *Zwingli and Bullinger* (Library of Christian Classics, SCM Press), 1953.

DeBold, R. C. and Leaf, R. C. (editors), *L.S.D.: Man, Drugs and Society* (Faber and Faber), 1969.

Dewick, E. C., *The Christian Attitude to Other Religions* (Cambridge University Press), 1953.

Eliot, Charles, *Hinduism and Buddhism* (Edward Arnold), 1921.

Geldenhuys, N., *Commentary on the Gospel of Luke* (Marshall, Morgan and Scott), 1950.

Goodman, George, *The Heathen. Their Present State and Future Destiny* (Pickering and Inglis).

Haggard, Rider, *She* (Longmans), 1887.

Hahn, Ferdinand (with Wenzel Lohff and Günther Bornkamm), *What can we know about Jesus?* Translated by G. Foley (St Andrew Press), 1969.

Hendriksen, W., *The Gospel of John.* 2nd British ed. (Banner of Truth Trust), 1961.

Hinnells, J. R. (editor), *Comparative Religion in Education* (Oriel Press, Newcastle), 1970.

Hocking, W. E., *Living religions and a world faith* (Allen and Unwin), 1940.

Hodge, Charles, *Commentary on I Corinthians* (Banner of Truth Trust), 1959.

Hooft, W. A. Visser 't, *No Other Name* (SCM Press), 1963.

Hume, R. E., *The World's Living Religions.* Revised ed. (T. and T. Clark), 1959.

Huxley, A., *Doors of Perception* (Chatto and Windus), 1954.

Huxley, A., *The Perennial Philosophy* (Chatto and Windus), 1946.

Hyde, L., *The Wisdom Religion Today* (Burning-Glass Paper, No. 13).

Islam, Encyclopaedia of (E. J. Brill, Leiden).

James, E. O., *Christianity and Other Religions* (Hodder and Stoughton), 1968.

James, E. O., *In the Fulness of Time* (SPCK), 1935.

Klostermaier, K., *Hindu and Christian in Vrindaban* (SCM Press), 1969.

Laski, H. J., *Reflections on the Revolution of our Time* (Allen and Unwin), 1943.

Lawrence, D. H., *Lady Chatterley's Lover* (Secker), 1928.

Lawrence, D. H., *The Man Who Died* (Secker), 1931.

Lewis, C. S., *Miracles* (Geoffrey Bles), 1947.

Lewis, H. D. and Slater, R. L., *World Religions* (C. A. Watts), 1966.

Lightfoot, R. H., *St. John's Gospel. A Commentary*. Edited by C. F. Evans (Oxford University Press), 1956.

Lyall, L., *Red Sky at Night* (Hodder and Stoughton), 1969.

Macdonald, D. B., *Muslim Theology, Jurisprudence and Constitutional Theory* (New York), 1903.

Masters, R. E. L. and Houston, Jean, *The Varieties of Psychedelic Experience* (Holt, Rinehart and Winston, New York), 1966.

Metzger, B. M., *Historical and Literary Studies* (E. J. Brill, Leiden), 1968.

Morgan, G. Campbell, *The Acts of the Apostles* (Pickering and Inglis), 1945.

Morgan, G. Campbell, *The Crises of the Christ* (Pickering and Inglis), 1945.

Neill, S. C., *Christian Faith and Other Faiths* (Oxford University Press), 1961.

New Bible Dictionary, The (Inter-Varsity Fellowship), 1962.

Newbigin, L., *The Finality of Christ* (SCM Press), 1969.

Nock, A. D., *Conversion* (Oxford University Press), 1933, reprinted 1961.

Oesterley, W. O. E., (editor), *Judaism and Christianity*, Vol. 1. *The Age of Transition* (Sheldon Press), 1937.

Oxford English Dictionary.

Panikkar, R., *The Unknown Christ of Hinduism* (Darton, Longman and Todd), 1965.

Pannenberg, W., *Jesus – God and Man* (SCM Press), 1968.

Parrinder, E. G., *An Introduction to Asian Religions* (SPCK), 1957.

Radhakrishnan, Sarvepalli, *The Principal Upanishads* (as quoted in H. D. Lewis and R. L. Slater, *World Religions*).

Radhakrishnan, Sarvepalli, *Recovery of Faith* (as quoted in S. C. Neill, *Christian Faith and Other Faiths*).

Ramsey, A. M., *Sacred and Secular* (Longmans, Green), 1965.

Richardson, Alan (editor), *A Dictionary of Christian Theology* (SCM Press), 1969.

Robinson, J. A. T., *Twelve New Testament Studies* (SCM Press), 1962.

Schaeffer, F. A., *Escape from Reason* (Inter-Varsity Press), 1968.

Schmidt, W., *The Origin and Growth of Religion*. Translated by H. J. Rose (Methuen), 1931.

Schweitzer, A., *Paul and his Interpreters* (Macmillan), 1912.

Shorter Oxford Dictionary.

Smart, N., *World Religions: a Dialogue* (SCM Press), 1960; (Pelican Books), 1966.

Smith, E. W. (editor), *African Ideas of God* (Edinburgh House Press), 1950.

Smith, W. Cantwell, *The Faith of Other Men* (New American Library, New York; New English Library, London), 1965.

Stace, W. T., *Mysticism and Philosophy* (Macmillan), 1961.

Stace, W. T., *Time and Eternity* (Oxford University Press), 1952.

Temple, William, *Readings in St. John's Gospel, First Series* (Macmillan), 1943.

Tillich, P., *Christianity and the Encounter of the World Religions* (Columbia University Press), 1964.

Webster's New Collegiate Dictionary.

Westcott, B. F., *The Gospel according to St. John*. Vol. II (John Murray), 1908.

Zaehner, R. C., *Hinduism*. 2nd ed. (Oxford University Press), 1966.

Zaehner, R. C., *Mysticism, Sacred and Profane* (Oxford University Press), 1957.

Zwemer, S. M., *The Influence of Animism on Islam* (Macmillan, New York), 1920.

INDEX OF BIBLE REFERENCES

GENERAL INDEX